Translating Christ

Translating Christ

The Memoirs of Herman Peter Aschmann
Wycliffe Bible Translator

HUGH STEVEN

WILLIAM CAREY
LIBRARY

Translating Christ: The Memoirs of Herman Peter Aschmann, Wycliffe Bible Translator

All scripture quotations, unless otherwise indicated, are taken from the Holy Bible, New International Version®, NIV®. Copyright © 1973, 1978, 1984 by Biblica, Inc.™ Used by permission of Zondervan. All rights reserved worldwide. www.zondervan.com

Published by William Carey Library, an imprint of William Carey Publishing
10 W. Dry Creek Circle
Littleton, CO 80120 | www.missionbooks.org

Brad Koenig, copyeditor
Francesca Gacho, editor
Rose Lee-Norman, indexer
Renee Robitaille, graphic design

William Carey Library is a ministry of Frontier Ventures
Pasadena, CA 91104 | www.frontierventures.org

Photo Credits: Photos in Chapters 4, 10, and 17 courtesy of Wycliffe Archives; Chapter 7 photo from author; cover photo and all other photos courtesy of Dan Aschmann.

Library of Congress Cataloging-in-Publication Data

Steven, Hugh.
  Translating Christ: the memoirs of Herman Peter Aschmann, Wycliffe Bible translator / Hugh Steven.
    p. cm.
1. Aschmann, Herman P. 2. Aschmann, Herman P.–Travel–Mexico. 3. Totonac Indians–Missions. 4. Totonac Indians–Religion. 5. Wycliffe Bible Translators–History. 6. Summer Institute of Linguistics–History. I. Aschmann, Herman P. II. Title.

ISBN: 9780878086191

23 22 21 20 19 Printed for Worldwide Distribution

Contents

Acknowledgments vii

Introduction ix

1. Please Tell Me What Happened 1
2. Misdeeds 9
3. Finding an Anchor 21
4. What Would God Think of That? 29
5. Discovering a New World 39
6. Jailhouse Rock 49
7. A Song for the Dead 61
8. Making Friends 73
9. Trying to Make Life Easier Doesn't Always Work....85
10. Accidents Will Happen 97
11. New Helpers 105
12. The Book That Smacked of the Truth 113
13. Fishing for Words.. 123
14. Born with Ink in His Veins 133
15. Give Me Your Soul 141
16. Please Never Come to Visit Me Again....................151
17. Thinking More of God's Past Blessings 161
18. A New Challenge 173
19. The Best Is Yet to Be.. 185

Afterword 195

Postscript...203

Appendix 205

Index..209

Acknowledgments

I first want to acknowledge and give my sincere thanks and appreciation to Herman's son, Dan Aschmann. It was he who gave me his blessing and encouragement to compile his father's memoirs into a narrative. For insights into Herman and Bessie's life and ministry I thank SIL colleagues Ruth Bishop, Dr. Ben Elson, and Dr. George Cowan, and former SIL colleague Dr. Dale Kietzman. I also express my appreciation to Felipe Ramos, Herman's language consultant and faithful Totonac friend.

I thank Ron Newberg, director of the Mexico Branch of the Summer Institute of Linguistics, for his encouragement and endorsement of this project. I also thank SIL colleagues Mae Toedter and Kathy Lehardy for their careful and helpful editorial suggestions and corrections.

My appreciation to Francesca Gacho, editor at William Carey Library, as well as the Library's General Manager, Jeff Minard, for their warm friendship and continuing interest in world mission. Special thanks to Brad Koenig for his careful copyediting and to Renee Robitaille for her creative cover design. I am also indebted to the Missions Committee of Trinity United Presbyterian Church in Santa Ana, California under the leadership of Laurie Jaworski (LJ) for their enthusiasm and financial support for this project. And to Barbara Wylie of Trinity's Wycliffe Prayer Committee who, for over forty years, has faithfully prayed for the many aspects of the ministry of Wycliffe Bible Translators.

To my wife Norma who has been a constant encourager, supporter, teammate, and editorial consultant, I here thank once again. Finally, I offer my profound appreciation to Herman Aschmann, who exemplified the dictum that one should look for the exceptional in the commonplace to find the unusual in the ordinary.

Hugh Steven
Santa Ana, California

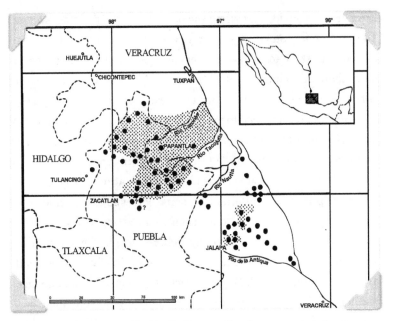

*Today, over a thousand indigenous churches are scattered
throughout the Totonac area in Mexico.*

Introduction

He was, as I always called him, a prince among men. His name was
Herman Peter Aschmann—friend, colleague, and Bible translator extraordinaire. When I began to write, I expressed an interest
in writing his story. Herman, with his wife Bessie, had produced an
early New Testament translation for the Highland Totonac peoples
who live in the eastern coastal and mountainous regions of the states
of Veracruz and Puebla, Mexico.

"Herman is, as you say, a remarkably dedicated and creative translator," said my colleague and writing mentor, Ethel Wallis, "but the
story of the Totonac work is the story of his co-translator, Manuel
Arenas. That's the story you should tell." In the providence of God,

I took Ethel's advice and wrote the book *Manuel*, and later *Manuel: The Continuing Story*. Beyond my wildest expectations, God used that simple story to inspire and encourage hundreds of readers in more than a dozen different languages. Additionally, *Manuel*, while currently out of print, went through seven printings. Now, just as good stories are supposed to make a full circle and end with how they began, it seems fitting to conclude my writing career with the story I first wanted to tell—the story of Herman Aschmann.

Over the years, I filed various bits of information I received from Herman's prayer or newsletters, personal correspondence, and notes from our private conversations. Then in 2002, six years before he died on his ninety-fourth birthday, Feb. 18, 2008, Herman sent me sixty-eight double-sided pages of his memoirs. His five married children—Rob, Tim, Rachel, Dan and Rick—together with their spouses had long before asked him to "sit down and write your memoirs." And write he did. After I read his account, I wrote Herman a letter expressing my reaction.

> As I read your story, it made me realize once again that God loves to choose the seemingly weak things in life to confound the wise in order to bring honor and glory to Himself. Uncle Cam Townsend was challenged by God to begin Wycliffe Bible Translators and the Summer Institute of Linguistics during the Great Depression, while he was still recuperating from TB. And for his teammate, Uncle Cam chose Mr. William G. Nyman, when he was weak with a heart attack, to become his wise Secretary-Treasurer and confidant. You, Herman, began your career, as most of us did, not entirely sure of who we were and wondering what talents or gifts we had that God could use. And now look, my dear friend, look what God has done through your skills as a Bible translator and your

loving kindness and courtesy that you and Bessie have given to the Totonac people. What a treasure you lay before the feet of our Lord! I loved your insight in your memoirs where you said, "I have come to the conclusion that God has a place for both my hang-ups and my strengths. If He likes us and made us that way, He knows how to use us that way." Spoken by a true prince among men.

Hugh Steven
Santa Ana, California

Johnny Aschmann.

1

Please Tell Me What Happened

The call—the kind no one wants to hear—came about an hour before midnight. Johnny, the nine-year-old son of one of our Bible translators, had drowned in a freak bathtub accident. His father, Herman Aschmann, was on a survey trip among the Highland Totonac people with photographer Paul Smith. Someone had to make an emergency trip that night to get the news to Herman of his son's death.

In 1959, the Mexico Branch of the Summer Institute of Linguistics (SIL) had several dozen translators living and working in remote villages scattered throughout the country of Mexico. Many of these areas were without paved roads, accessible only by air on marginal airstrips or by long days of hiking on narrow trails. To provide the translators with food, medicines, and other supplies required the services of someone who was centrally located. The buyer purchased the supplies requested by the translators and sent them to their families as quickly as possible. I was that person.

On that particular day I had been extremely busy. After fighting the frenetic and unpredictable Mexico City traffic, I arrived home to our small apartment greatly fatigued and retired about 10 p.m. For an hour I slept as if I had been drugged. Our friend and colleague Danny O'Brien, who lived in the apartment above us, had received the phone call. He banged on our bedroom window, and I awoke as if coming out of a deep well.

To this day I am not sure why my colleague Dick Blight and I were asked to find Herman and bring him back to Mexico City. We began our journey about midnight. I was driving my car. We traveled east out of Mexico City on the highway to Poza Rica and the low-lying market town of La Ceiba (named after a large tree by the same name growing in the town square).

I had been to La Ceiba several months before and knew there was a landing strip (which was just a field) and a bush pilot who served the rugged, mountainous Totonac area.

We arrived in La Ceiba about 6 a.m., just in time to surprise and wake up our fellow SIL colleagues Ruth Bishop and Aileen Reid, who worked among the Xicotepec de Juarez (at first called "Northern") and Patla-Chicontla Totonac people. Ever hospitable, Aileen and Ruth gave us an oatmeal breakfast. Herman and Paul had visited them two days before and shared their plans, so they told us roughly where Herman and Paul might be. "You will need to fly to the village of Coyutla," said Aileen. "From there you will have to hike up into the mountains to the village of Mecatlan, and if you miss them there, you will need to hike even higher to the village of Amixtlan."

The road off the main highway to the La Ceiba airstrip was nothing more than a rutted, grass-covered path. After parking my car up against a vine-covered, chest-high stone fence, Dick and I made our request known to the "ticket agent" of our desire to fly to Coyutla. The plane, an ill-kept two-seat Piper Cub, was just leaving on a quick trip to an interior village. The runway was short, and the bush pilot took off like he was in a great hurry.

I later learned that my assumptions were correct. La Ceiba sits at the foot of high mountains and deep canyons.[1] In the early afternoon, unstable winds develop in nearby canyons that make flying conditions unpredictable and dangerous. So the bush pilots hurry to get in as much flying time before noon as possible. About twenty minutes later, the red Piper Cub returned, taxied to a stop, and the pilot beckoned us to get aboard. Years later Dick related how it was that I, at 6' 2" and then about 160 pounds, and Dick, not much smaller, somehow got into the plane.

> The pilot was in the front seat. Then you (Hugh) backed yourself into the single back seat and squeezed over as far as you could. The pilot then put a low wooden block in on the floor of the plane. I then squeezed in so as to sit partly on your seat and partly on the block in the front of the seat. To say the least it was crowded when we took off for the twenty-minute flight to Coyulta.

When we arrived at the semitropical town of Coyutla and saw the steep range of mountains looming up from the base of the town, it became immediately obvious with Herman and Paul's two-day head start we could not possibly catch up with them. Further, even though we were young and reasonably fit, we were no match for these fearsome mountains. What we needed was a Totonac "runner"—someone who could find Herman and deliver the note that Dick typed on a battered typewriter in the town hall telling him about his son's death.

---

1 The road to La Ceiba was then a narrow, two-lane highway with several hours of hairpin turns and switchbacks that left the most seasoned driver with a queasy stomach. The final descent from the town of Villa Juarez, at about 3,000 feet above sea level, to the lowland town of La Ceiba, at about 300 feet, could be equally unsettling to one's equilibrium.

Like in most small towns or villages, and particularly in rural Mexico, two tall gringos (foreigners) generate great interest and speculation. And like bees drawn to honey, we soon had hangers-on who quickly knew our mission. In the providence of God, among the men gathered around us was a mule driver who had passed Herman and Paul on the trail as they climbed to the village of Mecatlan.

The man was about to make a return trip up the mountain to Mecatlan and was willing to deliver our note to Maria Lopez, a woman everyone knew. The instructions were that Maria would then send a runner up the trail Herman and Paul had taken to catch up with them and deliver the note. Years later, Herman recalled that incident.

> Like Hugh and Dick, Paul and I flew out of La Ceiba to the pretty town of Coyutla with its glistening meandering river and steep mountains rising from a flood plain. After we hired a carrier to carry our baggage, we spent the night in Coyutla and early the next morning we started our long trek up into the mountains. Paul wanted to photograph the colorful Totonac people, especially the women, who like many ethnic people, wore beautifully embroidered blouses and skirts, many of them homespun.[2]
>
> Our plan was to go first to Mecatlan and then hike still higher to Amixtlan. When we arrived in Mecatlan, we stopped to have lunch with Maria Lopez. She was the one whom God used to open up that Totonac village to the gospel. On the day we arrived, the men were away working in the fields. But when the women in the village learned I was there, they came flocking to talk to me. Many brought their

2 A Totonac woman is especially colorful with her white *rebozo* (scarf or stole) worn over a white blouse with fine red, green, blue, and yellow embroidery. The men at that time wore unbleached cotton shirts and trousers, often tied at the ankle. Many wore palm-leaf homemade sombreros.

sick children and asked me to pray for them. I was more than happy to do this.

After we had refreshed ourselves, Paul and I continued hiking the steep trails by way of Santo Domingo, Jopala, and Osorno until we reached Bienvenido. I knew this was a good town in which to spend the night since it had an inn the mule drivers used. At nine o'clock, just as we were ready to retire, I was surprised by a visit from one of the believers from Mecatlan. At first I had no idea why he had come from such a distance in the dark. He then handed me the note and my heart sank. The note contained no details only that Johnny had died and was now in the arms of Jesus. It said that Hugh and Dick were waiting for us in Coyutla and would drive us back to Mexico City as soon as we could make it down the mountain.

As devastating and shocking as this news was, I knew we had to get some sleep before we could retrace our steps back to Coyutla and then to the city. Thankfully, we were dead tired and were able to get a few hours sleep. About one a.m. in pitch blackness we began our descent with Paul, and several believers who met us in Mecatlan with mules.

Dick and I had arrived in Coyutla on Saturday midmorning. After giving the note to the mule driver, time was heavy on our hands. We spent the day trying to beat the heat with a swim in the river and drinking cold bottles of soda. The luxury of ice was trucked in over an unpaved road that was accessible only by trucks with a high wheel axle. On Sunday we waited and prayed the mule driver had delivered the note to Maria Lopez and that she had sent a runner who had intercepted Herman and Paul. It was unclear how Herman knew where to find us, but since there was only one hotel in town, the selection was probably obvious. In any case, about noon on Sunday, Herman, Paul, and four or five Totonacs who accompanied them met us at our hotel. What happened next is something I have remembered with great clarity, amazement, and admiration for more than fifty years.

The first thing Herman did when he found us was to greet us and then immediately turn to the Totonac men to make sure they had money to buy food and lodging for the night. He then turned to the mule drivers and the mules to make sure they had food and water. Only then, when the Totonac retinue was fully comfortable and their needs satisfied, did Herman turn to us and say, "Now please tell me what happened."

When I reflected on that incident, what struck me so powerfully was that this man of great humility could incarnate and affirm, in the most unlikely and unexpected of circumstances, the essence of true Christian servanthood. Later, Herman recounted the trip out of the area.

> In Coyutla we found there was no way of notifying the bush pilot in La Ceiba we needed his services (although Hugh and Dick had asked the pilot to come back for them on Sunday afternoon). With only a modicum of faith, we sat on the air strip for most of the afternoon to see if a plane would arrive. None did. We then decided to hike the nine or ten hours out to the highway.

What Herman failed to mention is that we began our "hike" in the back of an old Fargo Dodge truck. We drove through the village to ford the river at its shallowest part. Along the way, the driver picked up seven or eight other passengers with their gear who also wanted to get to the highway, until we were all crammed together like a bundle of upright asparagus stocks. After thirty-five or forty minutes of delay, we were on our way, only to be stranded midstream as we tried to ford the river. The ever-resourceful driver found a large leaf, wrapped it around the carburetor, and cranked the starter several times before the engine coughed to life, and we once again headed toward the highway. However, our hopes for a successful journey were dashed when—after an hour or so of crawling up and over earth berms, around potholes, and across bumpy cordwood tracks laid down in swampy areas—the truck sustained a broken axle.

After that, our journey became a comedy of errors. We were able to hitch a ride on another truck that was overloaded with coffee, only to have that truck also break down. By now we were out of the thick jungle and had reached a large, open plain. The moon was full, and it seemed bright as day. After walking for over an hour, we came to a small ranch. Some of the men in our party knew the rancher owned a Dodge Power Wagon. My Spanish then was limited, but I recall the men in our party were offering the rancher almost anything he wanted if he would drive us to the highway. After much persuasion and pleading and bargaining on a price, the rancher finally agreed to our request. We had been traveling—walking, in and out of trucks, and more walking—for almost nine hours. When at last we reached the highway, I was bone weary and flopped down on the side of the road and fell into a deep sleep. Herman described our trip to Mexico City.

> We got to the highway about midnight and after a half hour or so we flagged down a bus that took us to La Ceiba. There we got into Hugh's car and drove the six or seven hours to Mexico City. All during those stressful hours of travel and waiting, my mind just wouldn't accept the fact that Johnny could have died. There must be some mistake. Was I dreaming or was it real? Finally, when we arrived home and they took me to see Johnny laid out in his coffin, I was so overwhelmed

with grief I could not stop crying. "Lord!" I cried. "How could you let this happen?"

*Wilhelm and Liza Aschmann with daughters
Elsie and Mildred, and sons Paul, William,
and their third son, Herman.*

2

Misdeeds

With the aid of a midwife, Herman Peter Aschmann, the third child
and eldest son of Herman Wilhelm and Liza Aschmann, entered the
world on February 18, 1914.[3] The birth took place in the family home

---

3 In all, the Aschmanns had five children—Elsie, Mildred, Herman, Paul, and William. In later
years, it was with pride that Herman said his sister Elsie (over his father's objections) became an
artist, Mildred became a competent business woman, and Paul became a "tough guy and a good
athlete." William (Willy), the youngest in the family, was remembered as the most kindhearted of
all the siblings.

at 329 Willet Avenue, Port Chester, New York. What is significant about this home birth is how, in the space of ten years, Herman's father and mother met, married, and moved to this small community thirty or so miles north of New York City on the Connecticut border.

In 1904 Herman's father took advantage of a once-in-a-lifetime opportunity to find a better life for himself in the United States. Thus, under cover of darkness, Herman Wilhelm Aschmann, a cobbler in the service of the Russian Royal Navy, jumped ship while docked in the port of New York. Fluent in Latvian, German Yiddish, and of course, Russian, Herman Wilhelm arrived in New York at the height of the European immigration. He instantly became yet another indiscernible immigrant flooding the streets of the lower East side of Manhattan. With that one bold, daring leap of faith, God's plan for the Totonac people of Mexico was inaugurated.

If part of Herman's father's daring decision to jump ship was to escape the political turmoil and intrigue in his hometown of Riga, Latvia,[4] Herman's mother came to America out of a different neces- sity. Born in 1883, Louisa (Liza) Bersin was one of five daughters born to Latvian parents in the village of Ventspil on the shores of the Baltic Sea. Liza's father, a kindly Baptist minister, and her mother were devout Christians and were as devoted to their daughters as they were to their parish ministry. Herman tells of the circumstances that resulted in his mother immigrating to the U.S.

> My mother almost never spoke about her life in
> Latvia. But occasionally, at the end of a long day when
> the house was quiet, she would give us a glimpse into
> her past. When she did, she talked about her father
> who took her on lovely walks along the pristine white

---

4 In 1905 a revolution that had been brewing for many years broke out among the Latvian people who were frustrated by continuing Russian rule in their country. Workers went on strike and peas- ants burned many manor houses, then owned by the Russians and Germans. The authorities reacted harshly and scores of Latvians were sent into exile in Siberia. See Amanda Aixpuriete's *Looking at Latvia* (Minneapolis, MN: The Oliver Press, Inc., 2006), 8.

unspoiled beaches of Ventspil. As they walked, enjoying the ever changing clouds and cool refreshing sea
air, they made a game of who could find the small
pieces of amber (or sunstone) that sometimes washed
ashore after a storm.

But then the joy in her voice would suddenly turn to
a great sadness. She told us how her father had taken
the whole family to Riga, the capital city, to be present
for the dedication of the Trans-Siberian railroad. It was
an historic occasion of a mighty engineering railroad
achievement. Everyone wanted to be present to see the
arrival of the very first train to make the long historic
journey from Vladivostok to Riga. My mother would
then wipe away a silent tear from her cheek as she continued telling us that somehow in the crowd, her father
was pushed in front of the oncoming train and crushed
to death. In that single horrific accident, the fortunes of
the Bersin family changed forever. Without an income
and with no social safety net for widows, Liza and three
of her sisters paid their way to New York with money
they had borrowed from families to whom they became
indentured servants.

It's not clear how many years Liza worked as a domestic servant to
pay back the money her New York family spent on her boat passage.
The length of time an indentured person took to retire his or her debt
varied from three to seven years. If a family followed the accepted
custom of the day, an indentured servant who had paid back their
debt to begin life on their own was given a gift of clothes and money
from the family they had served. In Liza's case, her time of servitude
must have been about three years.[5] Herman wrote that with the aid

---

5 After Liza's three sisters left Latvia with her, one went to Canada and married a farmer. One went

of a matchmaker, his mother and father met at the New York Latvian Baptist Church about 1908 and married shortly thereafter. With the decision to marry came the responsibility to provide for his wife. And in the finest tradition of what it means to be an American,[6] Herman Wilhelm used his own ingenuity and talents as a cobbler.

> After my father and mother were married, they moved to Port Chester, New York. There my father earned his living as a cobbler. He would go from house to house asking people if they had shoes that needed to be repaired. After repairing the shoes, he returned them to the owner. After many years of hard work, my father became prosperous enough to start his own shoe store. He called it "The Aschmann Shoe Company." I always thought the name was interesting since he alone was the "Company."

Like thousands of Americans in the twentieth century, Herman's father was caught up with the unbounded confidence in the future of the country. By a stint of hard work and astute investments, the Aschmann Shoe Company prospered enough for Herman's father to build a new and larger home for his family. He also took a trip to Holland by steamship to visit his brother. By 1928 Herman's father had enough discretionary income for him and Liza to fly from New York to San Francisco to visit Liza's sister Anna and her husband August. It was a trip Liza had long anticipated. But her joy was shattered when she learned Herman almost died while she was away. On the eve of his parents' departure for California, a boil on the back of

---

to California and married a railway worker, and the third went to Brazil with a colony of Latvians. Over the years Liza maintained contact with her sisters in Canada and California but lost contact with her sister in Brazil.

6 In the 1900s, with the country rapidly expanding on all fronts, many new immigrants found jobs in the city, the coal mines, and as steel workers. Further, it was a time when it was no longer necessary to be Anglo-Saxon or Nordic to be considered an American. When Herman Wilhelm applied for citizenship, his lack of entry papers into the U.S. was somehow overlooked and he, like thousands of others, took the oath of allegiance and became an American citizen.

Herman's neck became infected. Over the next couple of days, the infection traveled down his right arm, swelling his arm to the point that the slightest movement caused him intense pain.

> There were no antibiotics. No one thought to take me to the hospital. By the time my parents returned, two places on my right wrist had become open festering pus-filled wounds. As I look back it was only by God's grace and mercy that I didn't die. For months I carried my arm in a sling. By the time it healed, two of the bones in my wrist had fused together. Bits of my wrist bone actually became detached and broke through the skin. This left my wrist with a bone permanently protruding. I truly consider that the infection healed by itself to be one of God's miracles.

It was entirely appropriate that Herman credited his healing to God. In 1928 Herman was a gangly, woolly-headed teenager who, by his own admission, was accident prone.

> My mom must have wondered about me because I was often sick. One of my earliest memories as a small child was of her holding and comforting me while she rocked me back and forth in an old rocker when I was sick or hurting from a fall. I thank God she never gave up on me. However, being accident prone must have been a concern for both my parents. I liked to climb trees with its accompanying bruises. I remember once falling from a tree in our front yard. As I fell, my clothes got caught on the spikes of the iron fence that faced the street. Another time, the boy next door threw a board with a nail in it that barely missed entering the white of my right eye.

I once jammed a large splinter of wood under one of my fingernails. It went in so deep there was no way to use a needle or pincers to get it out. I should have been taken to the hospital, but my dad felt competent enough to operate. I remember how much it hurt as he cut away part of the fingernail to finally take out the splinter. The result was a permanently misshapen fingernail.

In winter we kids did a lot of ice skating. One winter, while skating on what we called "rubber ice," I fell through. Rubber ice happens in early spring as the ice gets progressively thinner. You can skate on rubber ice as long as you keep going, but if you stop or fall you can easily break through the ice. And that's just what happened to me. Thankfully I broke through the ice close to the edge of the water. It was also good that Mrs. Lane, my Sunday-School-teacher, lived close by. Since it was too cold for me to go home in my wet clothes she took me to her home to get me out of the cold. Even though they were too big for me, she gave me some of her husband's clothes to wear.

And speaking of ice skating, I once had a pair of racing skates that had the front and back part of the blade sticking out beyond the skate shoe. As I raced around a sharp turn with a wall at the end of it, my left skate hit the wall. My right leg followed after it with the back of the blade driving right into the fleshy part of my right leg. I carried a deep scar from that accident for the rest of my life.

Like most young boys, Herman loved to fly kites and make things. In fact, Herman somehow managed to collect a good set of wood-carving tools and was constantly making things out of wood. One of Herman's projects was a set of stilts. And to his surprise, he learned to walk on them with great agility, even being able to walk up and down the front steps of his house.

> On the last pair of stilts I made, I put the foot rest more than a yard above the ground. On the foot rest I nailed a pair of old shoes. After I put my feet into them, and had snugly tied the shoestrings to the top of the stilts, I then strapped the lower part of my legs to the top of the stilts to free my hands. I also made some black pants to put on that reached to the ground. Someone saw me walking that way and hired me to walk around town advertising their store.

> But being me, an accident had to happen. One of my pant legs became entangled and I went crashing to my knees. I am sure God was with me, because there were no broken bones. However, when my father heard of my stilt escapade, he came home to see if I was hurt. When he saw that all I had were a few bruises, he promptly tore my stilts to pieces. I never walked on a pair of stilts again.

Happily Herman's father, or "Pop" as his children called him, seemed rather long-suffering about Herman's misdeeds. But there was one occasion when Herman exhausted his father's patience.

> I was still a small boy, but even small boys can create unforgivable disasters. One day I was showing off my pitching ability when I really didn't have any. But that didn't stop me from trying. Somehow the rock I was using for a ball left my hand and went the wrong way and crashed through the plate glass window of a store.

That time Pop gave me such a whipping I couldn't sit down for a long time. Even my two older sisters felt sorry for me.

Attention Deficit Hyperactivity Disorder (ADHD) may well have been the cause of Herman being accident prone.

I sometimes blame my ADHD for my many accidents and for being easily sidetracked. This happened not just when I was climbing trees. It also happened when I tried to verbalize my thoughts. It irks me when I keep leaving things out when my mind seems to think I've just said it or written it down. I have a problem of letting my thoughts get ahead of what I'm actually trying to say. When this happens, I've made a habit of trying to hide my confusion. Unfortunately this didn't always succeed.

In school, my mind was always racing and I was easily distracted. As such, my school work suffered. Even, as an adult, and as much as I try, my mind still wanders. I still find it hard to pay attention to what others are saying. Yet at other times I find myself so deeply engrossed in something that captures my attention nothing can distract me from it for long periods of time.

I wondered if God could ever use a person like me. In retrospect I must conclude that God has a place for both my strengths as well as my hang-ups. I know God has already used me just as I am and I knew He still will. All of us are unique.

God made us the way we are. And if he likes us that way, He knows how to use us with all our strange idiosyncrasies.

The story of the whipping he received from his father for breaking the plate glass window was always followed by Herman's recollection of how he related to his father.

> Although he almost never physically punished us, there was something about my father that demanded our obedience. No matter how much we did to please him, he didn't seem to know how to thank us, nor did he display any intimacy with us. He never hugged or played with us or showed any interest in our achievements. And he never praised us for the good things we may have done. As an adult I remember the night I was awarded my Boy Scout[7] Eagle badge. He didn't even attend the ceremony. That really hurt.

> On the other hand I too was insensitive to the subtle things he did for me. In about 1931 or 1932, he bought a new Model A Ford that had just come out. He never used it for himself, but took time to teach me to drive. He then put the car in my name. Pop and I went on a couple of long trips together. When it came time to renew the insurance, I didn't have the money so Pop put the car back in his name and insured it himself. As I thought about that incident, I have no idea what was in his mind. I know his intentions were good because he still let me use the car, but he just didn't know how to deal with it.

If Herman's father didn't know how to deal with his son, the family didn't know how to deal with their father's growing alcohol addiction. Curiously, he began to drink during the 1919 influenza

---

7 Herman believed his Boy Scout activities, outings with his troop, strenuous hikes, long-distance swimming in Long Island Sound, and ice skating in winter were valuable preparation for the rugged life he would one day live among the Totonacs.

pandemic when millions of people died around the world. In fact, more people died from the influenza than died in World War I. Somehow Herman's father got the idea that if he drank some wine or other liquor every day he would be immune from the flu. Always enterprising, Herman's father began making his own wine. And during Prohibition, he made his own brandy from a homemade still in his basement. Herman remembers the first time the effects of his father's clandestine activity affected him personally.

> I remember our cellar was full of barrels of wine and wine-making equipment. One day when I was around ten or so I found myself in my father's wine cellar. On one of the shelves were some small bottles of elder-berry wine. I took the cork off one of the bottles and took a swig. It tasted sweet and I drank some more. When I went upstairs, my mother saw I wasn't my normal self and asked me what I was doing in the cellar. When I told her, she surprised me with her violent reaction.

> My mother was the kindest and gentlest of woman and I owe a lot to her gentle ways. But my father's drinking was a terrible burden to her. So I am sure her anger over what I had done was out of fear that I might become an alcoholic like my father. I never forgot my mother's strong reaction to my wine tippling and it has stayed with me all of my life.

> What has also stayed with me over the years was how unpredictable my father was and how we were never sure where we stood with him. When he wasn't drinking he was a very capable person. But all that changed when he began drinking, which usually started in the afternoon. As an adult I can still remember my

feelings of sadness mixed with fear waiting for him to come home at night. I had the front attic room as my bedroom. With my bedroom window open I would stay awake in bed listening, waiting and wanting him to make it home safely. As much as I wanted to fall asleep, I couldn't until I would finally hear him climb up the steps and come into the house. As a family we all loved Dad. He had many likable ways, but his drinking made him do things he shouldn't have done. Worst of all we just didn't know how to help him escape from his addiction.

As Herman grew older and began working Saturdays in his father's shoe store, as did his sisters, he experienced a certain despair and despondency from never knowing how he stood in his father's eyes. But there would come a moment when Herman's heavenly Father left no doubt that Herman's standing before God was love, forgiveness, and joy.

*The spontaneity of Herman's life-changing decision to follow Christ
gave him a new freedom and vision that would one day change
the lives of a nation of people.*

3

Finding an Anchor

In 1932 eighteen-year-old Herman Aschmann made one of the biggest and most far-reaching decisions of his life. In his own words, Herman said, "I want to finally make sure of my eternal salvation." Herman's father rarely attended church services except for Christmas and Easter. Herman's mother, on the other hand, had a sincere Christian faith and saw to it that her children regularly attended Sunday School and church. She also made sure the children had something to put in the offering plate.

I have only pleasant memories of my church and Sunday School experience. The Sunday School teachers in the Baptist Church where we went every Sunday with my mother were loving and kind. I remember they faithfully taught from the Bible and made the gospel story of salvation through Christ very plain to us. Yet, somehow it never sank in. Then one Sunday afternoon I happened to listen to Percy Crawford's radio program. He was a youth evangelist and his theme centered on how there was nothing God wanted more than to forgive us if we would only let Him.

If anyone needed and wanted to be forgiven that afternoon it was me. I was dissatisfied with the direction of my life and with some of the things I was doing. I wanted to be a better person. I experienced a lot of tension because I never knew where I stood with my alcoholic father. Also I often got into trouble when I worked in my father's shoe store. That afternoon as I listened to Percy Crawford's message I realized more clearly that it was for my sins that Christ had died. I asked God to forgive me. I tearfully accepted and thanked him for doing that. I sincerely wanted Him to take control of my life and to change it.

There is a mystery to the spiritual experience known in evangelical circles as the new birth, or being born again. In some cases when an individual has a spiritual rebirth experience, there is an overnight character change. Old habits and unhelpful practices fall away, and there is an instinctive desire to trust God. In other cases, change comes less easily. It often takes time for the Holy Spirit to confirm that an individual has indeed been given a new life in Christ.

But what is not often understood is that people who have a new birth experience are babes in the faith. Thus they will need mature friends and mentors to support them as they begin their faith journey. And that's exactly what happened with Herman.

Days after that special afternoon when I gave my life to Jesus Christ, I began to doubt whether I had what it took to really carry through with my commitment to Christ. As I struggled with my self doubt and old feelings of inadequacy, I was thankful that God was patient with me. Little, by little I began to see it was God, and not me, who was going to change my life. I just had to let him do the changing. Happily I was able to talk to my mother about what was taking place inside me. But it was it different with Pop. I was afraid to talk about the things of the heart with him. I did make a few attempts, but it was awkward going.

One weekend he and I went to Stony Brook, Long Island to hear a famous Bible teacher. On the way back we didn't talk much about what we heard. I could sense he didn't think much of the speaker or the message. On another occasion Pop and I went to visit my mother's relatives, the Brydes, who lived in Appleboxville, Pennsylvania. Their son John saw my interest in spiritual things and started sending me material about a Pentecostal Bible School in Illinois.

On the way back from that trip, we visited another Latvian family who lived in New Jersey. One of the boys in the family was an enthusiastic Christian who liked to talk about Christian things. I liked that. Gradually Pop was beginning to see that something good was happening to me.

Shortly after my conversion experience, Shavarsh and Alyce Topazian, a Christian Armenian couple took an interest in me. They invited me to come to their home on Sunday afternoons to meet with a small group of young people for Bible study and fellowship. Their love and desire to see me grow in Christ was real and came at just the right time to help me find my way as a newly born again Christian. I owe so much to them.

I once went with them to visit a Bible school in New York City. This made me begin to ask myself if going to Bible school might help me. We also went together to Percy Crawford's spiritual life retreat in New Jersey. It was a wonderful experience. I blended in well with the enthusiasm of so many joyful Christian young people.

In spite of, or perhaps because of his ADHD, Herman had done well in his high school science and math. As he considered his future, he expressed an interest in attending MIT (Massachusetts Institute of Technology) to study mechanical engineering. However, when his father learned of his son's plans, he immediately said an emphatic "No!"

This was a time in American history when higher education wasn't held in high esteem by the work-a-day world. It was the self-made man (like Herman's father) who was admired most. In fact, some businessmen were suspicious of higher learning, believing it filled one's mind with extraneous knowledge and therefore hindered concentration on the main business of making money. Herman often wondered why his father had such a misguided notion that getting a college education wasn't worth it. He speculated it was because his father had, by his own hard work, pulled himself up by his bootstraps and made a success of himself without a higher education.

I think he wanted his children to have had the satisfaction of doing the same. Or was it that he wanted to keep his children home with him in order to keep the shoe store in the family?

I remember how, as children we all had to work in the store. He even paid us by the day to be there selling shoes. On top of our tiny day wage, he paid us a 5% commission for any shoes we sold. Pop tried to teach us how to save the money we earned and had us open our own savings account at our local bank. While my sister Mildred worked as his bookkeeper, my other sister Elsie wanted to go to college. She wanted to be an artist and planned to take classes at City College in New York City. When Pop learned about her plans, he ridiculed the idea of her thinking about such a foolish thing and told her not to go. However, Elsie was of age and simply left home and moved to the Big Apple where she worked her way through City College. After receiving her diploma, she worked as a commercial artist for over fifty years.

Without financial or moral support from his father, Herman's dreams of an MIT education were dashed. However, he did have the support of his Armenian friends, Shavarsh and Alyce, and they suggested he consider going to Bible school. In 1934, at age twenty, Herman decided that tuition-free Moody Bible Institute[8] in Chicago would be a good place to study and prepare himself for whatever the Lord had planned for him. Since Herman's personal finances were limited, and a school that offered free tuition was enormously attractive, the choice for Moody seemed obvious. Yet there was another equally compelling reason for choosing Moody. The school was in

---

8 Moody Bible Institute was named after its founder, the great American nineteenth-century evangelist, D. L. Moody.

Chicago, far from his home in Port Chester and the stifling influence of his father.

> If I had chosen a Bible school closer to home, my father may have come and forced me to come home. At the time I was working fulltime in the shoe store. I knew Pop was grooming me to one day take over the shoe store business. My fear was he would try and keep me from going to school. And I was right. When I told him about my plans to go to Moody, he became so angry that he did the unpredictable. He told me to leave home and not come back until I had changed my mind. Thus it was with a heavy heart that I left home and went to stay with some friends.[9] I had very little money of my own when I boarded the train for New York City and then on to Chicago. Fortunately, my mother's parting gift was her blessing and a hundred dollar bill which she sewed on to the inside of my undershirt so I wouldn't lose it. As the train pulled away from the station, I knew I was doing the right thing, and yet as much as I tried I wasn't able to completely free my mind from feelings of guilt that I was disappointing my father.

To help pay for his living expenses at Moody, Herman worked at a number of different jobs. He first worked as a painter. Next he bused tables at several downtown restaurants. But the best paying job was working nights at the Burlington Railroad freight depot. Herman said the pay was good, and he saved enough to buy a Model T Ford, which enabled him to drive home between semesters. There was, however, a drawback with having to work nights. He lost a lot of sleep, and his grades suffered.

---

9 The pain of this experience never left Herman. Years later, when his Totonac co-translator, Manuel Arenas, was likewise forced by his father to leave home because of his new faith in Christ, Manuel found an empathetic welcome in Herman and Bessie's home in the village of Zapotitlán.

It's not clear how or under what circumstances he and his father were reconciled. Herman wrote that when he took his first semester break and drove home in his new Model T Ford, he and his father were "somewhat reconciled." However, Herman was quick to note this fragile truce didn't mean he was able to enjoy a more intimate fellowship with his father. Further, Herman's sense of guilt for disappointing his father by not working in the shoe store was never completely free from his mind, or from the conversation of some of the store employees.

> One of the salesmen in the shoe store once scolded me by saying my father needed me and I shouldn't have deserted him. This was hard for me to hear and I began to sense how sad my Pop must have felt when I went away. Once again doubts surfaced in my mind about whether I had done the right thing by going to Moody. But then an inner voice (I believed was the Holy Spirit) assured me that I had made the right choice.

Years later, as Herman reflected on his relationship with his father, he admitted he never knew what his father was like on the inside. He also admitted as an adult his thoughts about his father had softened, and he was more empathetic over the things he did and why he was the way he was.

> I like to think of him now as a man like myself, insecure yet so willing to keep taking risks. The difference between us was that I found an Anchor, someone to go to for help. He didn't. The only way he knew how to handle his insecurity was to drink his way through. I often wondered why, with the light he had been given from my mother's simple faith, he did not go to God for help.

The nature of a personal memoir is to remember fragments of one's life that were especially meaningful and poignant. In 1938 there occurred such a moment for Herman. As he prepared to return to Moody on his last visit home, both his mother and father came to the railway station to see him off.

> It was a great surprise to me when my father said he was coming to the train station to see me off. He may have wanted to say some words of encouragement to me, but he didn't say much. I think he just didn't know how to put his inner feeling into words. In March of 1938, my father at age fifty-eight died of prostate cancer. When my father realized he had cancer, he began to talk to my mother about eternal things. I like to think it was through my mother's sincere faith that he was finally reaching out too. Pop asked her to read to him from the huge leather-bound Latvian Bible my mother had inherited from her father. My mother also said that Pop would also sit with her and listen to her favorite gospel radio programs.

Shortly before Herman's father died, Herman received the one and only letter his father ever sent him. It was a short, handwritten note telling Herman that he wanted his son to know that he now realized how far he had wandered from God. He said he had asked God to forgive him, and he knew God had heard him as he put his trust in Christ to save him. He then asked Herman to forgive him.

> As I thought about my father, I thought this is a sad story with a happy ending. The good part will come later when some day I will meet Pop in Heaven. There we won't be able to hide anything from each other. We will all have lots to tell each other of God's undeserved kindness to us on our earthly journey.

Camp Wycliffe, 1938
Front row, from left, #1 - Bill Bently, #3 - Herman Aschmann.
Second row, from left, #4 - Elvira Townsend, Townsend's first wife,
#5 - Cameron Townsend, #7 - Evelyn Griset, Townsend's niece
who later married Ken Pike.
Third row, from left, #4 - Eugene Nida, #6 - Ken Pike.

4

What Would God Think of That?

It came as no surprise to Herman that his ADHD often caused him to adjust an action or reevaluate the direction of his life. When he graduated from Moody's pastoral course, in December 1937 he had serious misgivings about entering the pastoral pulpit ministry.

> I thought long and hard about whether I should become a preacher. Whenever I tried to speak in front of an audience, my ADHD gave me problems. This made me realize that preaching was not my gift.

But then I wondered what my next step should be. The answer came from listening to a variety of missionaries who came to speak to us at Moody. The more I listened to them the more I became convinced the next best thing for me to do was become a missionary, and I wondered what God would think of that. So, with that in mind, I stayed on at Moody to take another semester of courses on missionary subjects.

One of the missionary speakers Herman heard at Moody was Leonard Livingston Legters, or simply L. L. Legters. Legters was a flamboyant firebrand missionary with a stentorian voice who, with a great sense of theater, challenged students to give their lives in service as a Bible translator to one of the many indigenous people groups in Latin America without the Bible in their own language.

Like his namesake, the Scottish missionary explorer David Livingstone, L. L. Legters called himself a pathfinder and missionary explorer. This was no idle boast. He had worked among the Comanche and Apache Indians in Oklahoma. In June of 1926 he, with an expedition of seven made an extraordinarily difficult language survey of the unprotected wilderness area of Brazil's Mato Grosso. This area, now known as Xingu National Park, was home to at least sixteen different preliterate ethnic people groups that included the warlike Chavante, the Tsikáo, the Cayapo, and more.[10] Herman wrote about how he felt after hearing Legters speak to Moody's student body in early 1938.

Mr. Legters wanted us to know there were over 2,000 unwritten languages[11] in the world that had nothing of

---

10   To learn more of L. L. Legters' survey trip to Brazil and the part he played in the formation of Wycliffe Bible Translators, see Hugh Steven, *Wycliffe in the Making: The Memoirs of W. Cameron Townsend, 1920-1933* (Wheaton, IL: Harold Shaw Publishers, 1995).

11   Cameron Townsend's understanding of the actual number of ethnic peoples without the Bible was based upon the best available information at the time. With the advent of more sophisticated survey data recording, the SIL Ethnologue data update of October 2006 lists 6,912 languages in the world. Of these, 2,403 have a complete Bible; 1,115 have an adequate New Testament; and 862 have portions of the Bible.

the Bible translated for speakers of those languages. He also wanted us to know about a new school called Camp Wycliffe.[12] It was a school started by William Cameron Townsend who had translated the New Testament for the Cakchiquel people of Guatemala. The purpose of the school was to give potential Bible translators the linguistic training they would need to learn and analyze an unwritten language.

Herman's account of Legters' high adventure in Brazil, was brief but, nonetheless gave the high points and reasons for his trip. Since there was no reliable statistical information available about the ethnic peoples of the Mato Grosso, Legters wanted firsthand information about the complexity of reaching the ethnic peoples of that area. After hearing how dangerous and demanding it would be to work in a country where it would take a month of river travel in an open canoe to reach an ethnic village, Herman thought that "translating the Bible for these aboriginal languages seemed too difficult for anyone to undertake." Yet after hearing Legters tell how he had met Cameron Townsend and how Townsend had learned the Cakchiquel language and translated the New Testament into that language, Herman came to a different conclusion.

When Mr. Legters asked if any of us would be interested in learning how to translate the Bible for a group of people somewhere so they could be reached for Christ, only two of us said yes, my friend Bill Bentley and I. The logic of translating the Bible for a Bibleless tribe appealed to me. At the same time, I wondered if I had the intellect to do that, let alone learn to speak and analyze an unwritten language. Bill Bentley felt the same as I did, but we finally decided maybe we should

---

12 Camp Wycliffe eventually became the Summer Institute of Linguistics.

risk it and let God be the one to show that to us. So
we both decided to take the course that summer. Mr.
Legters told us Camp Wycliffe was going to be held in
the old Presbyterian[13] camping grounds near Siloam
Springs, Arkansas.

When Herman boarded the Greyhound bus that took him to
Siloam Springs, little did he realize this forward step of faith would
lead him into a Bible translation ministry that would span more
than half a century. Herman did not comment about his bus trip,
but he did wonder about going to a school that began in 1934 with
only two students. Remarkably, much had changed in five years.
The obligatory Camp Wycliffe class photo of 1938 showed a group
of thirty-one students and staff with one babe in arms. In 1938, two
students who became teachers at the school, Kenneth L. Pike and
Eugene Nida, were on the cusp of getting their doctoral degrees.
They would later gain recognition as world-class linguistic scholars.[14] After Herman stepped off the bus in Siloam Springs, he
hoisted his duffel bag over his shoulder and went looking for the
house of Dr. Blast, his contact person.

In 1934 Cameron Townsend and his first wife Elvira arrived in the
Ozarks seriously underweight and in need of physical restoration.
Cam believed the calm, clean country air of the Ozarks would be of
immeasurable help in restoring their broken health. Cam's prediction
proved correct, but it was more than clean air that provided the anti-
dote. Much of Cam and Elvira's return to good health was due to the
professional and personal care of Dr. and Mrs. George Blast. In fact,
to better treat and care for the Townsends, the Blasts invited them to
be their houseguests. Over time the good doctor, like so many others,
caught Cam's vision for Bible translation and happily volunteered to

---

13 Other sources said it was the Baptist camping grounds.
14 For further information about the 1938 Camp Wycliffe, see Hugh Steven, *Doorway to the World,
The Mexico Years: The Memoirs of W. Cameron Townsend, 1934-1947* (Wheaton, IL: Harold Shaw
Publishers, 1999).

help in anyway he could during the weeks the linguistic school was in session.

> I had been informed that Dr. Blast was the one who would take me by car to the Baptist camping grounds where the school was to be held. When I finally located Dr. Blast's home and rang the door bell and was greeted by the good doctor, he kindly informed me I had arrived two weeks early!
>
> My problem now was what I would do and where would I stay for the next two weeks. I then remembered that the previous summer I had gone with a carload of fellows from Moody on an evangelistic trip to a rural church near Tahlequah, Oklahoma. This was a small town about fifty miles from Siloam Springs. We fellows had been billeted with a family that had a big farmhouse near Tahlequah, Oklahoma. I thought, "Why not risk it and go back to the family that had put us up during the evangelistic trip to see if I could stay with them for two weeks?"
>
> I left my duffel bag with Dr. Blast, and off I went hitch hiking to the town of Tahlequah. When I arrived, the farm family was more than happy to have me as their guest. To help this stranger feel less guilty for imposing on them, they even put me to work. Two weeks later I finally arrived at Camp Wycliffe where new adventures awaited me.

One of the curious hallmarks of the early Camp Wycliffe experience was its rustic accommodations. The first school in 1934 was held in an abandoned schoolhouse overrun with vines and grasses on what was then called Happy Valley Farm. A commonality of Camp Wycliffe when Ken Pike attended the school and when Herman attended in 1938 was the noticeable lack of furniture in the classroom.

> That old Baptist camping ground was composed of a cluster of shacks nestled in a wooded area. There was very little furniture. A longtime friend of Mr. Townsend, Tom Haywood, who owned a hardware store in the nearby town of Gravette, supplied us with quantities of empty nail kegs that we used as chairs. Our teacher, Ken Pike, had used the same nail kegs when he first attended Camp Wycliffe. Besides the nail kegs, Tom Haywood kept us supplied throughout the long very hot summer with sweet watermelons. He also supplied us with chickens that he often barbecued for us. We students and teachers all ate together and took turns as cooks. Some of us didn't do too well at that.

One of Herman's fellow students that summer was Evelyn (Evie) Griset, Cameron Townsend's niece (who would later marry Ken Pike). In a letter home, Evie told how she and Herman were the camp stewards for that week. She said it was the steward's job to buy the food and see that everyone had enough to eat but not to go over budget. However, Evie said there were several dietary problems to consider. One lady could not eat protein. Uncle Cam's wife Elvira could not eat starch, and Uncle Cam objected to the cabbage they were serving and could not eat pickles. Said Evie, "So you see it's a great life. Herman and I changed the menu so much that week it became a common joke." But what wasn't a joke was the way Herman felt about that first summer at Camp Wycliffe and the linguistic training he received. When I wrote *Wycliffe in the Making: The Memoirs of W. Cameron Townsend, 1920-1933*, I asked Herman to tell me how he felt about that summer. He described his feelings and first impressions.

When I first met Cameron Townsend in 1938, I didn't have good feelings about my abilities. The little I learned of linguistics that year was indeed little. But there was something about that summer of study that rang my bell. I wanted to know more. We students all needed someone to make us feel we could do something hard like learning unwritten languages and translating the Bible into those languages. Cameron Townsend ("Uncle Cam," as we all came to call him) was the one who had the gift and heart to do that. Uncle Cam helped me and others to activate our faith and imagination to try hard things for God. He was always going out on a limb [of faith] which made me uncomfortable and yet things worked out right in the end. He seemed to think anybody could do anything if God were in it. And we believed him. I think we believed because of the way he listened to unimportant people like me. I sometimes wonder what would have become of me if my life hadn't been challenged by this man's vision.

Dr. Ben Elson, former Mexico Branch director and one of Herman's good friends, helps us understand why Herman went with Uncle Cam to Mexico at the end of that first summer of linguistic training.

Uncle Cam had the ability, as do all great leaders, to bring out the best in the men and women he led, to lead them forward toward the goals they believed were important, yet without violating their own individuality. His leadership was marked by a deep personal concern for others. He always had a smile, an attentive ear, a word of encouragement and support. I remember him as having a forgiving, compassionate attitude toward those under his leadership.

For many of the students at that 1938 summer session, the end of Camp Wycliffe was the beginning of their linguistic and Bible translation career. And as he had done since 1934, Uncle Cam caravanned with a group of would-be translators to Mexico. Herman and Bill Bentley were two of ten people who made the trip at the conclusion of the summer. When the group first crossed the border at Laredo, Texas, Uncle Cam showed the immigration officers the letter from President Lázaro Cárdenas in which he had personally invited Cam to bring into the country as many young people as he needed who were willing to help the indigenous groups of Mexico. In the minds of the immigration officers, this was such a strange and improbable letter that they delayed the group for several hours while they phoned Mexico City to check its authenticity. When they finally confirmed that President Cárdenas had indeed written the letter and invited Cam to bring in as many young people as he needed, they sent the group on its way to Mexico City without checking their documentation. However, they instructed them that their papers would be checked in the immigration office in Mexico City. Herman now faced a dilemma.

> I don't think any of us newcomers had passports. But the officials in Mexico City said all we needed was a birth certificate. Since I didn't have one, I hastily wrote my sister Mildred in Port Chester, New York where I was born to get me one and send it to me as quickly as possible.
>
> To my surprise I learned my birth had never been registered. However, my ever resourceful sister found the very midwife who had delivered me. With her in hand, plus my two sisters, they went to the Port Chester

office where babies are registered and vouched for my existence. The proper official then made out a belated registry of my birth. When I received the copy of my new birth certificate, I was surprised to see that my sister had given me the middle name of Peter which I had never had before.

All travelers know about unexpected delays and disrupted schedules. Under such conditions many people can become irritable, frustrated, rude, and demand their rights, but not Uncle Cam. From long experiences in Latin America, he showed the utmost courtesy to the officials he spoke to at the border. And it was this display of courtesy, kindness, patience, and God-likeness in dealing with one's fellow human beings that was forever imprinted on a young Herman Aschmann during that border delay.

During that long night when Dick Blight and I hiked with Herman to reach the highway in the company of some rough Mexican men, I saw that Herman exhibited the same God-likeness to these men as his mentor Cameron Townsend would have. Later the Mexico Branch assigned Herman the job of securing important government documents, renewing Mexican visas, and dealing with government officials at all levels. It was a position that required the ability to read, write, and speak Spanish well. And it required the skill of a seasoned diplomat. Herman was known for being one of the best at his job.

A historian—observing Cameron Townsend starting out for Mexico City driving an old Hudson; another car packed with idealistic, first-time linguists; and Verne Bruce, Cam's "field man," driving a sidecar motorcycle—might think they were all tilting at windmills. But Cameron Townsend was no Don Quixote; he was a visionary. He had seen the practical outworking of his vision in Guatemala. This included growing, indigenous church; a Bible institute; a school for girls and a trade school for men who wanted to learn carpentry, shoe repair, barbering, and other useful trades.

The uniqueness of Townsend's vision was his confidence in God's promises that when you seek to purposefully obey and do God's will He acts in ways far beyond your dreams. Thus, believing God would honor his step of faith, however weak, Herman began his trip to Mexico City with just seven dollars. To save money, he slept by the side of the road. Yet his tiny flicker of faith inspired by his mentor would bring about an enormous transformation in the lives of untold thousands of people.

Hubel (Lem) Lemley and Herman,
fellow students at the 1938 Camp Wycliffe.

5

Discovering a New World

"A journey," said Northrop Frye, "is a directed movement in time through space that requires two elements. One is the person making the journey and the other is the road or path."[15] For Herman the first steps in his career journey began with his decision to attend Camp Wycliffe in 1938. It had been a summer of intellectual and spiritual stimulation. For the first time Herman was exposed to the science of descriptive linguistics. From his teacher, Ken Pike, he discovered

---

15 Northrop Frye, *Myth and Metaphor: Selected Essays, 1974-1988* (Charlottesville, VA: University Press, 1996), 212.

that learning to speak an unwritten language would be easier if one had an understanding of phonetics and phonemics (the study of a language's sound system).

When Herman's other teacher, Eugene Nida, was teaching him the techniques for analyzing the grammar of an unwritten language, he said, "It is ridiculous to assume that so-called primitive, or aboriginal languages are devoid of grammar. Speakers of such languages do not just throw words together. All languages have word order rules and a pattern. Our job as linguistics is to find that pattern and catalogue the rules just as we do in English."

In addition to learning about morphology, syntax, and phonemics, Herman also had courses in basic cultural anthropology. Here he became aware of the different customs and cultures of aboriginal peoples. He learned that an understanding of the cultural implications of an aboriginal language were necessary for a meaningful translation of the Bible.

At the end of the summer, Herman was all the more convinced God had directed his choice to attend Camp Wycliffe. Further, the idea of translating the Bible for a Bibleless people, which was first implanted by L. L. Legters at Moody, burned even brighter. This was especially true after he heard Nida say, "Relatively few missionaries have undertaken the task of exploring the strange sounds and strange words and even stranger meaning [of an unwritten language]. But those who have made this journey have a marvelous story to tell." Nida went on to say, "The journey into the secret realms of a people's language introduces one to the soul of a nation and makes it possible to lay the foundation for teaching the Truth as it is found in the revelation of God through the [translated] scriptures."

While Herman believed God directed his career journey, he had chosen a path (for the best of all reasons) that could lead him away from service with Wycliffe. Despite L. L. Legters' dark assessment of how difficult it would be to work in Brazil, Herman applied for mission service to the Amazon Indian Mission. However, God's chosen path for Herman would lead not to Brazil, but to Mexico. And the instrument God chose to bring this about was a fellow student.

During that 1938 Camp Wycliffe, Herman became close friends with Hubel Lemley ("Lem" for short), a fellow student and one of Uncle Cam's recruits who volunteered to go to Mexico with him in the fall. One day Uncle Cam showed Lem a letter (in Spanish) from the town secretary of Tlacoapa, in the state of Guerrero, Mexico. Originally the letter had been sent to the Mexican Bible Society. But since the letter was a plea for someone to come and teach the Bible to the large number of Tlapanec ethnic people in the area, the Bible Society sent it to Uncle Cam. When Cam read the letter to Lem, he considered it to be God's leading for him to translate the New Testament for the Tlapanec people. The only problem—Lem didn't speak Spanish, nor did he have a coworker to go with him. Since Herman could speak a little high school Spanish, Lem asked him to be his teammate and go with him. Herman told Lem he was a good friend, but that he planned go to Wheaton College in the fall. Further, Herman had applied to the Amazon Indian Mission to work in Brazil. Lem said he understood, but by the end of the summer he had persuaded Herman to spend a year working with him among the Tlapanec people in the state of Guerrero. And that is how Herman found himself with nine others in the caravan on their way to Mexico City.

> All of that happened after Uncle Cam presented the letter written by the President of Mexico, Lázaro Cárdenas, inviting us to work with Mexico's Indian people. After the officials at the border verified the letter was authentic, we began our journey. In those days the road from Laredo to Mexico City was mostly unpaved. It was a dusty slow drive as we made our way around burros and cattle that shared the road with lumbering trucks on a two-lane road with little room to

pass. We spent the first night in the city of Monterrey. The one and only tourist motel before reaching Mexico City was in Tamazunchale. Happily we stopped there for the second night. The next day we started our climb up through the mountains. However, before we reached the valley of Mexico, we had to sleep one night in our sleeping bags on the side of the road.

When the caravan finally reached Mexico City, there was a collective sigh of relief. To his surprise, Herman found this mile-high capital city of up to four million people[16] ringed with the famous snowcapped mountains of Popocatepetl (the mountain that shakes) and Ixtaccihuatl (Sleeping Lady). A writer who first viewed these mountains before the days when Mexico City became filled with lung-choking smog said, "Both of these mountains rise from maguey and cornfields above which their snow-crested peaks seem to float like two white wraiths. By day they stand upon a gray-blue haze, but at the setting of the sun their summits and the sky are mingled in shades of delicate pink and lilac."[17] Herman was at last happy to arrive at their destination.

What a relief to arrive in Mexico City. In those days there were no traffic jams, no smog, and almost no tourists.

He discovered broad, tree-lined boulevards like the famous Paseo de la Reforma, built by the Emperor Maximilian in the mid-1800s to have a direct and beautiful route from Chapueltepec Castle to the government buildings off the Zócalo (the central square in downtown Mexico City). In addition, there were exquisite cathedrals, elegant fountains, inviting plazas, and classical structures of all kinds to see.[18] As inviting as these new sights were to explore,

---

16 As of this writing, the population of the oldest, continuously inhabited city in the Western hemisphere tops twenty million.

17 John A. Crow, *Mexico Today* (New York: Harper & Brothers, 1957), 3.

18 Joel Poinsett, first ambassador to Mexico, 1825–1828 (and namesake of the poinsettia flower,

they would have to wait, partly because Herman arrived in Mexico City with limited funds.

I remember only having seven dollars with me when we crossed the border into Mexico. A month later my mother started sending me twenty-five dollars a month. She was the first one to begin helping me with my support.[19] Later, as I wrote friends telling them about my new career, others also began supporting me. For the entire life of my career there was always some money that came for me (and later for our family). Often it was very little, but we would-be Bible translators were all poor in those days.

One of the other ways we were able to stretch our money when we first arrived was through the many friends Uncle Cam had made. Mr. Marroquin, the director of the Mexican Bible Society, offered us single fellows (Bill Bentley, Hubel Lemley, Bill Sedat and Ken Weathers), a spare storage room in which to keep our belongings and sleep at night in our sleeping bags.

The single girls (Mildred Kimmel, Carol Jackson, Mildred Kuntz, Josephine Nikkel, Evelyn Griset, and Lois Stephens) all stayed with Mrs. Hull, an American lady, in her big old mansion of a house. The married couples also stayed there. They were Otis and Mary Leal, Brainerd and Eva Legters, Walt and Vera Miller and Newell and Elsie Stickney. Some of the wonderful

which he introduced to the United States), wrote that Mexico City was one of the most opulent metropolises in the world (over 70,000 people) with broad streets, impressive public buildings, fine parks and plazas, and lavish mansions. "The streets are well-paved and have sidewalks of flat stones. The public squares are spacious and surrounded by buildings of hewed stone and very good architecture. There is an air of grandeur in the aspect of this place." Gerard Helferich, *Humboldt's Cosmos* (New York: Gotham Books, 2005), 282.

19 Every Wycliffe worker, including Mr. Townsend, had to raise their own financial support. Usually this came from a sending-church foreign budget and from interested friends and family.

friends we met during those early days included Mr. Webb, who everyone called Daddy Webb, a tall Englishman who imported British-made products that included woolens and bicycles. Mr. Peasley represented the Singer Sewing Machine Company in Mexico, and Mr. Ingram, was an independent English missionary. These two Christian business men had their offices in Mexico City.

While Herman noted living in the Bible Society's storage room was a godsend, he was quick to say most of the people were soon on their way to their tribal locations. Bill Bentley went to the state of Chiapas to work with the Highland Tzeltal people. Six of the new members went with Uncle Cam and his first wife Elvira to the Aztec village of Tetelcingo, about a hundred miles south of Mexico City,[20] where Uncle Cam and his wife were themselves working.

As always Cam was eager to improve the economic fabric of the community in which he served, and was cooperating with a government-sponsored agricultural program directed by Professor Uranga. Actually it was President Cárdenas—now Cam's good friend—who, at Cam's suggestion, put Professor Uranga in charge of this experimental station as a way to help the Aztec people in this village. Finally, with Verne Bruce as their guide, Herman and Lem took off to spend a year working with the Tlapanec people.

Verne Bruce, while never an official member of what was then called The Townsend Group, nevertheless liked what we were doing and helped many of us get settled in our tribal locations. Verne Bruce had traveled extensively in rural Mexico and was just the right person to allocate many of the earlier translators.

---

20 See the many references to this village in Hugh Steven, *Doorway to the World, The Mexico Years: The Memoirs of W. Cameron Townsend, 1934-1947* (Wheaton, IL: Harold Shaw Publishers, 1999).

And now he was getting Hubel Lemley and me settled among the Tlapanec people of southern Mexico.

In December, we took off on a narrow gauge train heading south for Chietla in the State of Guerrero. From there we traveled by foot with a mule that carried our belongings. It took us two days of hard hot walking to get to Tlapa, Guerrero where we stayed for five days. There we finally found a mule driver who, with his mules, would take us and our baggage the three walking days to the village of Tlacoapa. However, in Tlacoapa, the town secretary, whose letter had been instrumental in leading Lem to go there, turned out to be a disappointment. To our amazement, he denied ever having written the letter. But here we were and Lem wanted to stay. So after getting acquainted with some of the town officials and looking around, Verne took us on a three-week backpacking survey trip through the Tlapanec-speaking area. We took only our sleeping bags.

In 1938 the science and technique for tabulating and identifying language families and dialects (now called variants) within a given language family was in its infancy. Yet before a translation program begins, the translator should know the geographic and linguistic boundaries of the language for which they will translate the New Testament. The question the survey team would try to answer is whether the New Testament translated for the people living in the immediate area of Tlacoapa would serve the needs of the people (with the same tribal name) who lived at a greater distance from Tlacoapa.[21]

What is remarkable about Herman's memory of that three-week

---

21 For example, Herman Aschmann's language survey among the Totonacs revealed the need for three separate New Testament translations—Highland, Papantla (Lowland), and Coyutla.

language survey is the absence of anything negative, hard, or unpleasant. Most survey teams report one or more hair-raising incidents. In 1922 L. L. Legters, with his traveling companion Paul Burgess, did a six-week survey of the languages in Southern Mexico. Legters, who was no stranger to pioneer living and rugged backpacking, reported that survey to be the most horrendous six weeks of his life. They were stoned, had little to eat, and got crippling blisters severe enough to require bed rest. And at the end of their trip, racked with fevers, they ended up in the hospital. The only incident on Herman's survey that he felt was worthy of including in his memoirs was a flash flood.

> After we returned to Tlacoapa, Verne left us. But not until he found an indigenous man who promised to take care of Lem and me on their family farm. We found a flat place on the slope of a mountain just above the people's huts, and pitched our pup tent Lem had brought along. It was a poor choice because a storm came up one day and that convenient flat place became a lake of water. It invaded our pup tent and soaked all our belongings. Fortunately we were in hot country and our things soon dried out and we again settled down to pup tent living.

Eduardo, the oldest son of the Tlapanec-speaking family living just below where Herman and Lem had pitched their tent, volunteered to work with Lem in analyzing his language. Eduardo also worked with Herman.

> Since I had the advantage of speaking Spanish, which Eduardo also could speak, Lem let me work with Eduardo. Before I knew it, my curiosity about the sounds and grammar of the Tlapanec language began to grow. It seemed like I was actually beginning to understand and distinguish the distinctive sounds of

the language so I could determine what letters to use in the orthography [writing system].

As Herman began to seriously study the sounds and grammatical structure of the Tlapanec language, something new, exciting, and profound began to be awakened in him. It is best summed up in words from a celebrated sermon by F. W. Robertson: "A few actions often decide the destiny of individuals because they settle the tone and form of mind from which there will be in life no alteration."[22] In Herman's case the "no alteration" would be his commitment and acute understanding of the sound and grammar system of the Totonac language. As yet, however, he was just becoming aware of his own potential as a linguist and Bible translator.

> Before I knew it, my curiosity about the sounds and grammar of the Tlapanec language began to grow. Day by day as I worked with Eduardo, the oldest son of the Tlapaneco family living below our pup tent, I was beginning to sort out the distinctive sounds so I could determine what letters to use for the Tlapaneco orthography. At Camp Wycliffe I had learned that this language, like any other, had its own distinct number of significant sounds or phonemes each of which could be given a letter in formulating its written alphabet. A linguist's job is to sort them out. Just think, here I was for the first time actually giving this language its own unique alphabet so that anyone could learn to read and write it in a consistent and unambiguous way. Working on a real language and getting somewhere encouraged me. It made me feel that this indeed was something I could enjoy becoming good at.

22 Stuart Barton Babbage, *The Mark of Cain: Studies in Literature and Theology* (Grand Rapids, MI: William B. Eerdmans Publishing Company, 1996), 55.

It soon became apparent to Herman that Tlapanec was a tonal language. Every word, or perhaps every syllable, seemed to have its own distinct tone level or contour. As proof of this, Herman said he happened upon two words with different meanings that were spelled the same except for the change of tone in which they were pronounced. When he discovered the change of tone in a word could also change its meaning, Herman was challenged to find out how many distinct tone levels there were.

> I soon figured out it must only have three tones, low, mid and high. Finding this out was for me like discovering a new world.

This new world of linguistic discovery would be for Herman, as for most Bible translators, a journey, as one writer said, "Of deep observation and a slow accretion of details." For Herman it would also be a lifelong, incandescent, joyous journey into the very heart, soul, and mind of the Totonac people.

Herman with Vicente Cortes, Tetelcingo, 1939.

6

Jailhouse Rock

It was clear to Herman that love was in the air for his friend Hubel Lemley and that he was anxious to return to the States. After spending almost six months studying the Tlapanec language, Herman and Lem returned to Siloam Springs for yet another summer of linguistic studies at Camp Wycliffe (now known as the Summer Institute of Linguistics). Among the twenty-two students of that 1939 class was Mildred (Millie) Lewis, a charming Southern belle from Memphis, Tennessee. Herman said Lem and Millie had been old friends, but before the summer was over, this casual friendship turned to romance, engagement, and marriage. With Herman as best man, Lem and Millie were married in September.

Knowing how advanced Herman was in understanding Tlapanec language, Lem and Millie persuaded him to return with them to Tlacoapa, Guerrero, which he did.

> That October the three of us returned to Mexico. Doing this conflicted with my previous desire to go to Wheaton College. I had also applied to the Amazon Indian Mission to work in Brazil. Having received no answer from them and with my heart strings drawing me back to Mexico, my conscience was relieved. I later realized that God was in my decision to return with them even though, at the time, I felt pulled in all three directions.

The first principle students were taught at Camp Wycliffe was that, to produce an accurate and meaningful translation, a Bible translator must work at all levels of the descriptive linguistic process. A translator must understand the phonology (sounds), the morphology (words, including inflection and tone), and the syntax (arrangement of words). These are prerequisites for producing an accurate translation of the New Testament in an indigenous language.

Millie, a natural mimic and attentive student, quickly absorbed all Herman knew of the Tlapanec language. In December Herman felt Millie had grasped enough of the basic framework of the language and decided to leave the newlyweds on their own. Eduardo had built them a thatch-roof hut that would serve them well for at least a few years. Herman then returned to the village of Tetelcingo where Uncle Cam and Elvira were working. Cam was pleased to have Herman back for a short visit, but Herman was more pleased because he wanted to ask him something. Herman had learned that because of ill health, Landis and Gerdis Christiansen, who had worked with the Totonac Indians of eastern Mexico, had to leave Mexico for good.

I wanted to ask Uncle Cam about the possibility of my taking the Christiansens' place among the Totonacs. With a happy smile and with his blessing Uncle Cam told me that indeed I could go. He said, however, that there was no one available to go with me. Verne Bruce had originally allocated the Christiansens in the Totonac village of Zongozotla. When I asked Verne how I could get to that village, he told me that town wasn't the best place for me to go. It would be better to try getting into the Totonac[23] area from the north, say from Lake Necaxa which is just below Tulancingo, Hidalgo.

When Hernán Cortés (the fair "god" from across the sea) conquered the Aztec Empire and emperor Montezuma II in 1519 and returned to Spain, King Charles VI asked Cortés to describe what Mexico was like. It is reported that Cortés took a sheet of paper, crumpled it, dropped it on the table, and said, "This, sire, is what Mexico is like. [A land of deep valleys and high mountains]" Herman Aschmann was shortly to discover firsthand exactly what Cortés meant by that crumpled piece of paper. Eager to begin his new assignment among the Totonacs, Herman made his way to Lake Necaxa.

In those days there was no car road going from Mexico City east to the mountainous country to Lake Necaxa. There was, however, a narrow-gauge rail line that went by a short distance above it on the central plateau of Mexico. And that's what I took. I got off at the place where there was a shuttle bus that took people a few miles down country to the lake and town

---

23 The Highland Totonac—with a population of 120,000—is one of the larger ethnic groups in Mexico. They live in the rugged, jungle-covered mountains in the northern part of the state of Puebla. Highland Totonac is one of the dialects (variants) of a family of languages that may have over 250,000 speakers.

of Necaxa.

In Necaxa, Herman found a mule driver and told him he wanted to go to a village where people spoke Totonac. The mule driver said he was about to go to the Totonac village of San Felipe Tecpatlan and offered to take Herman there.

> This was great! So off I went again, this time by foot, with my duffle bag on top of the load of one of the mules. The next day we traveled through the mountains to the town of Tlaola. On the second day we finally reached the town of San Felipe Tecpatlan. It was dark and raining when we arrived. The mule driver unloaded his mules in front of the only store in town. I couldn't understand anyone except the storekeeper since the rest only spoke to each other in Totonac. I introduced myself and asked him if there was a place I could stay. He took me to the next room and showed me a corner where I could sleep. I was dead tired and it didn't take long before I was sound asleep in my warm and cozy sleeping bag. But then I was suddenly jolted awake by the screams of a woman and a man yelling at her in the next room. He must have been beating her. I felt so helpless and wondered what was coming next. Finally they quieted down and I was so tired that I went right back to sleep.

The next morning, Herman introduced himself to the town president. However, it soon became apparent this village did not welcome strangers. The president didn't say Herman couldn't stay, but he suggested it would be better if Herman went to another town to study the Totonac language. The president said there was no place in his town where he could stay unless he wanted to use one of the two jail cells as his abode. With no other option, Herman took his offer. At Camp

Wycliffe, Herman was taught the best way to learn an unwritten language was to find a native speaker who would become your friend, teacher, and language mentor.

> I tried sitting on the bench in front of the jailhouse to see if I could find a passerby who would be willing to help me learn their language. No one wanted to talk. So I wandered around town to find somebody who could speak some Spanish. That wasn't too successful. I had little more success sitting in front of the town hall where a few men often gathered to visit. But that didn't work well either. I soon saw how hard it was going to be to find the words and phrases to start a Totonac dictionary and learn the language!

Not only was it difficult for Herman to find someone to help him learn the language, finding food to eat was also a problem.

> Happily there were some huge mango trees nearby. They were loaded with fruit much of which was falling to the ground without being gathered. I like mangos and soon had my fill of them and then some. There were also oranges and bananas piled up at the store that were waiting for people to buy and take to the market town to sell. Those I could buy. But one can't live on fruit alone. What I lacked was someone who would make a decent meal. I did have some oatmeal and a little gasoline cook stove. But I ate my oatmeal so often it soon was gone.

> An interesting thing happened one day in the jailhouse. They had locked up someone in a cell next to mine and were keeping him there without feeding him. The custom in those jails was that it was the obligation of

some relative or friend to feed any imprisoned inmate. This poor fellow didn't seem to have anyone to do that for him. One day he pleaded with me to get him something to eat. I said I would and went out to buy him some fruit. But when I returned, to my surprise he was gone. He had somehow climbed to the top of the wall and escaped into the jungle. That was possible because the two jail cells had no ceiling and the loose tile roof made it possible for him to push the tiles aside and squeeze his way over the wall and get out.

A short distance from Herman's jailhouse, there was a little, ancient Catholic church. But when Easter week came, Herman saw no activity in the church until Good Friday. On that day he said he saw many women going inside.

I then heard the women chanting something they must have memorized in Spanish. Suddenly I could hear all of them crying and wailing as loud as they could. They sounded so real in their sorrow over Christ's death on the cross I wanted to see what they would do on Easter Sunday. To my surprise not a soul showed up at the church on Easter Sunday. Then I happened to look off in the distance to where I saw some men on a hillside cultivating their fields. This made me wonder why the death of the crucified Christ meant so much to them while the resurrected Christ hadn't made much of an impression. I thought about what might happen to these needy people if God would allow me some day to translate the New Testament for them. I wanted to believe that many lives would be changed when they found out what God really wanted them to know about Christ's death and resurrection.

Not many years later, that is what God let happen among those Highland Totonacs. What is remarkable about Herman's next entry in his memoirs is the length of time he spent in this uncomfortable and unfriendly town. With uncharacteristic criticism he said:

> After four miserable months [in San Felipe Tecpatlan], I came down with a severe case of malaria. No one came to help me and in a few days I was seriously sick and in no shape to walk out to Zacatlan to get help. That was the closest town, where I could catch a bus to Puebla or Mexico City. If God had not sent a friendly mule driver along with an empty mule for me to ride, I don't know if I would have made it out alive. In Zacatlan I caught a bus to Puebla where I went to see Dr. Dawson, our missionary doctor friend at the Baptist Hospital. After a few weeks of recuperation, I made my way back to Tetelcingo and Uncle Cam Townsend.

While it may be a simplistic cliché that says, "Our disappointments are often God's appointments," it was certainly true for Herman when he returned to Tetelcingo.

> There a delightful surprise awaited me. When the Christiansens left the Totonac village in which they had worked to return to the States, they invited a Totonac man to come with them to Tetelcingo. His name was Vicente Cortes. He spoke Spanish and Totonac, which made him an excellent Totonac language teacher. Uncle Cam saw that Vicente loved flowers and hired him to be his gardener. He also introduced him to Martín Mendéz, the town president

that Uncle Cam had led to the Lord.

Just before I arrived, Martín Mendéz had led Vicente to the Lord. When we met, I told him about the difficult reception I received in the town of San Felipe Tecpatlan. Vicente didn't hesitate a moment to suggest I go to his home town of Zapotitlán. Although his mother was a widow with five children living with her, he assured me she would take me under her wing and allow me to live with them.

Although Herman had misgivings about these living arrangements, he made his way to Zapotitlán, Puebla, one of the most northern of all the Totonac villages. Herman didn't know how Vicente got news to his mother that he would be coming to Zapotitlán, but when Herman arrived, Vicente's mother and her family were happy to welcome him.

The family lived in a large, one room stone house with just one bed. At night I slept in that bed and the three boys slept on mats they laid down on the floor. Their names were Marcos, Pancho and Fulgencio. Filomena, the mother, slept outside under the lean-to kitchen with her two daughters Ester and Lupe.

The town of Zapotitlán sits beside a swift river with towering mountain ranges on either side. The townspeople leave each day to work in their fields, some of which are quite a distance from the village. Like everyone else, Filomena had her plot of land that was on the steep side of a mountain, a half-hour walk from their home. Filomena knew Herman needed a teacher to help him learn Totonac and designated Fulgencio to stay at home to teach him. The children could speak Spanish, but Filomena couldn't. This meant that while Herman was part of that household, Totonac was what he heard and what he immediately had to try to speak.

> To state the obvious, for a foreigner, six people all living
> together in a one room house had its drawbacks. There
> was no running water, no electric lights, and no out-
> house. For the latter there was a convenient patch of
> woods behind the house where one could go and be out
> of sight. The hardest thing for me to get used to was the
> lack of privacy. But what an ideal way to learn Totonac!
> I can't remember exactly. But I must have spent six
> months or so living in Zapotitlán with that loving family
> during the latter part of 1940 and the first part of 1941.

In 1940, at age twenty-six, Herman was in full, youthful, physical vigor and had the tousled hair of a linguistic adventurer. Besides
his interest in learning all he could about the Totonac language and
culture, Herman loved to hike. At age sixty-two, Herman took a
young twenty-something Jim Watters (who would one day become
the Mexico Branch director) to his first language allocation. When
they started out over the long, hard mountain trail, Jim wondered if
Herman would be able to keep up a steady pace. But, as he reported at
Herman's memorial service, "This old guy could hike circles around
me and not be fatigued." Herman's hiking ability was, of course,
conditioned from many years of hiking some of the muddiest and
steepest mountain trails in all of Mexico. Yet it didn't deter him from
exploring the Totonac area.

> Being young and in good shape physically, I thought
> nothing of getting away for a few days to just hike from
> one village to the next. In that way I got to see many
> of the Totonac villages. On two different occasions I
> hiked all the way down to Papantla where Lowland
> Totonac is spoken. The Totonacs there dressed differ-
> ently and spoke a different variety of Totonac that I

had trouble understanding.

When Herman was living in San Felipe Tecpatlan and became ill with malaria, he left his duffel bag packed with all his clothes. Herman's new friend Marcos said he would be glad to go with Herman and backpack it for him to Zapotitlán.

> It took us half a day to hike there. When we arrived I found to my surprise the jailhouse was in ruins. I was glad I had left my duffel bag in the care of the town president instead of in my jail cell, which was now a pile of rubble. San Felipe Tecpatlan sits on a steep slope right at the base of a tall cliff. Occasionally rocks would become detached and come tumbling down onto the edge of town. While I was away, that's exactly what happened. A huge boulder came crashing down and plowed right through the jailhouse, completely destroying it.

Herman didn't mention in his memoirs that the huge boulder could easily have crashed into the jail while he was sleeping there. God had surely protected him during the months he lived in the jail. Herman continued his account of that long and interesting hike.

> For that hike with Marcos I had purchased a pair of Indian sandals to wear instead of my shoes. The soles of the sandals the Indians wear were cut out of old worn out car tires. They punched three holes in them through which they pushed the thongs and then knotted them underneath. The thongs then were wrapped around one's ankle. On our way to Tecpatlan I had no trouble with them as they were quite comfortable. There was however, a problem about them I hadn't anticipated, namely, when the leather thongs get wet

they stretch. On our return trip home, we were caught in a downpour. Soon I could no longer keep the sandals on my feet. The soles of Indian feet were callused and tough. Mine were tender. I had to more or less hobble gingerly home barefooted the rest of the journey. That was the first and last time I wore their kind of sandals.

That summer Herman discovered something else he was never to wear again—bachelorhood.

A young Totonac man takes time out to read from his Totonac New Testament.

7

A Song for the Dead

Curiously Herman's memoirs show no indication he was waiting for love or was interested in the opposite sex. Even when he first met the attractive Bessie Dawson, the woman who would became his wife, Herman was noncommittal.

While he was living in the Totonac village of Zapotitlán, Herman had collected a large amount of raw language data he needed to analyze. He also had many questions to ask Vicente Cortes, his new friend and language teacher. The best place to do this was away from the activity and demands of village life.[24] In the summer of 1940,

24 In the early days of SIL in Mexico, there were no designated places where a translator might spend

Herman spent a few months in Tetelcingo where he had Vicente at his disposal to work with him on the language. Later he went to Mexico City for a few weeks, and it was there he met Bessie Dawson. At first Herman didn't pay much attention to her, until he heard her sing.

> She had a most beautiful bell-like quality to her voice and I was captivated. From then on I felt she was a person I would like to know better.

In 1941 Herman took a third summer of linguistic training at Camp Wycliffe, where his interest was not always on language study.

> Somehow Bessie and I became more and more attracted to each other. I had plenty to tell her about my exploits with the Totonac Indians, but I doubt whether that was what impressed her most about me. It was just a case of mutual attraction. Within a month we were engaged. Since Bessie's parents lived in Berkeley, California, they wanted her to be married in their home church. Before the summer was over, we were on our way to California.

Herman and Bessie were married on August 16, 1941, at Westbrae Bible Church in Berkeley, California. Herman was twenty-seven, Bessie twenty-five. Almost immediately the newly married couple returned by train to Mexico with the mutual vision of translating the Bible for the Highland Totonacs.

> In those days, getting to the village of Zapotitlán was hard. You first had to take a narrow gauge train from Mexico City to the city of Puebla where we stayed overnight. The next day we took another little train

---

several weeks or months in concentrated, uninterrupted language study, research, and translation. It wasn't until the 1960s that the translation and workshop center in Ixmiquilpan, a hundred miles north of Mexico City, was established for this purpose. In the meantime, while Mr. Townsend lived and worked in Tetelcingo, he welcomed those who needed a place to work on their language data.

with wooden cars that took us to Zaragoza, Puebla. From there we went by taxi on a dirt road to the market town of Zacapoaxtla. At about 6,000 feet above sea level, Zacapoaxtla is located in the rugged mountains east of Mexico City on a plateau that drops abruptly into the Gulf of Mexico. It can be extremely cold and wet in the higher elevations of those rain forest mountains. And that exactly describes the village of Zacapoaxtla. It is also where the car road ends and the jumping-off place for travel by foot or horse north to where many Totonac Indian villages begin. To reach Highland Totonac country, we had to contend with bitter cold, and search for mule drivers to take our things, over impossibly muddy trails. What better honeymoon could one ask for! In those days it was a twelve-hour trip on mule back or by foot from Zacapoaxtla to Zapotitlán, our destination. The trail goes over some of the roughest terrain imaginable.

Filomena was happy to meet Bessie and even happier when she heard her use some of the Totonac phrases Herman had taught her. Bessie was such a good mimic that Filomena exclaimed: "Why she speaks better Totonac than Pedro does!" (The name people knew Herman by in Mexico was "Pedro" and Bessie became "Elisa.")

Across the street from Filomena's house was an empty stone house that belonged to Miguel Manzano. He was happy to let us live there. However, there was no furniture so we newlyweds had to wait for a carpenter to make us a bed. We did bring an air mattress, which was quite comfortable even when there was only the ground on which to put it. We also had a little gasoline cooking stove. I have to say those first few days were

very inconvenient. But then our lives changed when
Miguel Manzano's wife, Aurora, took pity on us and
somehow got Miguel to let us live in two rooms of his
mansion of a house.

Miguel was a *mestizo* and one of the wealthiest men
in town.[25] Miguel had built a sprawling collection of
large rooms, most of which were empty or used as
storage rooms for a multitude of things. He was an
ingenious blacksmith as well as a banker, merchant
and large landowner. His father had been a general in
the Mexican Revolution on the rebel side.

Aurora supplied us with furniture. Our kitchen was a
lean-to that faced a patio overgrown with weeds. And
to our happy surprise we discovered an outhouse with
a flush toilet. Miguel was an imaginative builder and
artisan. He constructed a reservoir on the other side
of the river where there was a spring. He then piped
water from the reservoir over the river right into his
house. He had the only running water in town.

Herman and Bessie soon realized Miguel and Aurora seldom spoke
to each other. She lived in two rooms next to them, while Miguel lived
like a hermit in the northernmost room with his blacksmith shop in
between. Over time, Herman and Bessie learned the tragic story of
their marriage.

Before Aurora and Miguel were married, he built
this large elegant house for his wife-to-be. However,
shortly after they were married, Aurora fell in love
with a flashy young mule driver and foolishly eloped

---

25 A *mestizo* is someone with mixed ancestry, especially someone in Latin America of both Native
American and European ancestry. Mestizos form the largest population groups in many Latin
American countries.

with him. After a few years, the mule driver left her and Aurora returned home repentant and wanting to live again with Miguel. He let her live in two of the rooms but would have absolutely nothing to do with her except for emergencies. She made his meals, but a maid took them to him in his quarters. Years later Aurora responded to the story of Jesus Christ's sacrificial love for her and she voluntarily gave her heart and life to follow the Lord as her savior.

Herman and Bessie found Aurora to be a kind and gentle person who befriended them in many ways. Miguel was quick to tell Herman he was an atheist. Yet he didn't mind talking to Herman about spiritual things. In spite of his cynicism about life (to him all humans were suspect), Herman showed Miguel unconditional love and accepted him as a friend. Because the two men were on good terms with one another, Herman and Miguel could engage on a variety of topics, including the nature of God's love for all mankind. Years later, Vicente Cortes told Herman that, toward the end of Miguel's life, Aurora's changed life did have some influence on him.

Years before we arrived in Zapotitlán Miguel purchased a Model T Ford that was now sitting in his blacksmith's shop with its engine removed. The tires were original and unworn. It seems in his younger days he had purchased the car new and somehow had driven it to Zacapoaxtla. From there, on a temporary road, he drove it to Zapotitlán. With all the rain, mud and impossible turns on the trail, I wondered how he could possibly have made it. But when he drove the Model T around town, it scared so many people and animals that the town authorities forbade him to drive it.

At that point, he took the motor out, learned how to start it with gasoline, and kept it running with kerosene. He then used it with a contrivance of pulleys to run his sugar cane press. Many years later during the 1970s, Bessie and I took a trip to Nanacatlan to be at Felipe Ramos' wedding. As we passed by Miguel's blacksmith shop in Zapotitlán, I noticed the antique car was no longer there. Someone must have seen this treasure and bought it from him.

Fulgencio, who was assigned by his mother Filomena to teach Herman and Bessie the Totonac language, worked with them faithfully every day. But one day Filomena needed all hands to work at cultivating and cleaning their field for planting. Their cornfield was—as is often the case in those rugged, overpopulated mountains—more like a cliff than a field. Tragically that day, Fulgencio fell off a steep place on the side of the mountain to the hard ground and rocks below. In the book *Manuel* I described that tragedy.

For three desperate days, Bessie worked to stop Fulgencio's internal bleeding. When she failed, the village priest suggested oil and vinegar as a "sure cure." This nauseating mixture immediately produced violent vomiting and Fulgencio died.

Almost immediately the church bells announced the event to the village, and Fulgencio's body was wrapped in a straw mat for burial. At the wake, Manuel Arenas listened and watched in amazed silence. Never before had the village of Zapotitlán experienced a Christian funeral. In a beautiful soprano voice, Bessie sang newly translated Totonac hymns. Vicente read a passage of scripture in Totonac.[26]

---

26 Hugh Steven, *Manuel* (Old Tappan, NJ: Fleming H. Revell, 1970), 38-39.

After Fulgencio died, another young Totonac teenager, living a block away from Herman and Bessie, presented himself to be the Aschmanns' teacher. His name was Manuel Arenas. Manuel offered his help primarily because he was curious and wanted to know more about the outside world. He had attended the town school for three years, as many other Totonacs had, and knew how to read and write in Spanish. Outside of school, however, he spoke mostly Totonac and worked daily with his father and brother in their fields. He knew Herman and Bessie had books in Spanish, and thought maybe the foreigners could teach him about the outside world. Manuel was also dissatisfied with the direction of his life. He wanted to be a good person but found it hard. He also wasn't satisfied with the Totonac notions and beliefs about the spirit world. The result was that he settled for being an intelligent skeptic with many unanswered questions and doubts about Totonac Indian animistic[27] beliefs and practices. Some of these were even connected with the established church. It's interesting to see how the Totonacs borrowed some of their symbolism, like praying to the statue of a saint so it would do things for them.

Incorporating prayer to statutes of saints fits with Totonac taboos and the interesting ways the spirit owners in nature could be manipulated. Historians tell us that four centuries ago the Totonac people helped Hernán Cortés in his conquest of Mexico. With Cortés' success in his conquest, the Totonac people were one of the first indigenous groups in Mexico to be systematically evangelized by the monks that followed the conquerors to Mexico. An ancient yet magnificent little Catholic church was built in Zapotitlán, as there were in many Totonac towns and villages. A monastery was also constructed to carry out evangelization.

---

27 Animism comes from Latin meaning breath or soul. It is a philosophical and religious concept that souls or spirits exist, not only in humans, but also in nature. An animistic view of nature holds that birds, animals, trees, mountains, rivers and other entities of nature have sprits. Animism also allows that such spirits can be outwitted, bargained or placated with sacrifices of various kinds.

Before the conquest of Mexico, the Totonacs lived in rural areas in the fields they cultivated, not in towns. In order to better evangelize them, the monks persuaded them to live in villages. Although the monks, with Totonac labor, built monumental stone churches in many of the villages, they were never fully able to control or erase the Totonacs' animistic notions and taboos. Totonacs believe that just about everything in nature has a spirit owner. To these spirit beings, the Totonacs just added the statues that also had something alive or magical about them that could be manipulated or appeased, just like the spirit owners of things in nature. The greatest leap in faith Herman and Bessie saw was when some of those Totonacs began to trust "in someone out there" whom they couldn't see, touch, or somehow symbolize in a material way.

> To think of someone who is everywhere as well as right next to them is just too mysterious to comprehend. Giving them the printed Bible in their language gave them access to that invisible Creator God.

One of Manuel's most troubling unanswered questions had to do with God as Creator. Most Totonacs believed that when God finished His creation He abandoned it and left it on its own. It would be several years before Herman had an adequate grasp of the Totonac language to explain to Manuel that, from the beginning, God's eternal power and divine nature are active in His creation, and that He did not abandon his creative handiwork.

Despite this background, Manuel's sense of wonder about his natural world caused him to believe the God of creation must still be interested in what He had created. Further, he believed God was "out there," and wondered what God was like and longed for someone to help him understand and explain his intuitive feelings. Herman was impressed that Manuel, as young as he was, showed an unusual sensitivity to wanting to live a life different from the accepted Totonac cultural pattern. It was a pattern that included working in one's corn-field, marrying, begetting children, and drinking sugarcane rum on the weekends. In most cases drinking is excessive, which leads them to a mestizo store owner who might overcharge them into signing their life away.

Herman would learn of Manuel's dissatisfaction and fear over the way so many Totonac men became alcoholics, which in turn often led to feuding, vengeance, and even killings. Instinctively Manuel under-stood that if he did not purposefully seek a better life, the cultural pressure in Zapotitlan would force him into the same downward cycle as virtually all the men in his village and in most every other Totonac village as well. And in the providence of God's grace, He heard the longings of Manuel's heart.

> From the beginning, Manuel came every day to study with me. He first supplied me with new words for the Spanish-Totonac dictionary we were compiling. I introduced him to a Spanish Bible and told him some of what was in it. I told him of our desire to translate the New Testament into Totonac and asked him if he would like to help us do that.

Manuel liked the idea, and he and Herman began translating some key verses that spoke clearly of God's offer of forgiveness and salva-tion through Christ. As Herman guided Manuel in his search for a meaningful translation of those individual verses, Manuel began to realize how they applied to him personally. That gave him a hunger to keep on translating. He even promised to stay with Herman until the translation of the whole New Testament into Totonac.

> With Manuel as translator and me as his consultant, we kept at it for twelve long years until we finished and had the Highland Totonac New Testament ready for printing.

Manuel knew that coming every day to study with Herman, instead of going to work with his father in the cornfield, would mean trouble. It came to a head one day when his father threw all of Manuel's belongings out on the street and told him he could return when he gave up these foolish notions. But rather than return home, Manuel picked up his belongings and went to live with Herman and Bessie. Manuel kept visiting his mother, but only when his father was not at home.[28]

What Manuel lacked in preparation for the task of translating the Bible was made up by his utter dedication. He told Herman more than once he wanted to quit but couldn't. God wouldn't let him! Also, he would never take payment for all the sacrifices he made to finish the New Testament translation.

During Manuel's early days of study with Herman, Bessie would sometimes be in another room singing Spanish hymns to the children who came to visit. Bessie had a little autoharp she strummed as she sang. Once when she was singing the hymn, "Come to the Church in the Wildwood," but with Spanish words, Manuel asked, "Why can't I translate the words of that song into Totonac?" Herman told him what the hymn implied and that he shouldn't try to translate the Spanish words literally into Totonac but compose new words around the same theme that would fit the timing and melody. That was all Manuel wanted to know.

> Before we knew it, Manuel had given us the words for the first hymn in Totonac. The Totonacs have a lot of folk music they play on their flutes. This is always accompanied by the beat of tiny drums. They also had many folk tunes played on their violins or guitars. Manuel felt these folk tunes were inappropriate to be sung with a Totonac message. In fact no one had ever used these folk tunes to accompany someone singing

28 For a further explanation of this event, see Hugh Steven, *Manuel* (Old Tappan, NJ: Fleming H. Revell, 1970), 52.

in Totonac. If they sang at all, it was only in Spanish. But the hymn tunes Bessie used were to him somehow appropriate for the message that went with them. When the children heard Bessie sing that first hymn in Totonac they wanted her to sing it again and again.

Teyo was one of the little boys who frequently came to visit Herman and Bessie. To their great sadness Teyo became ill and died. To venerate their dead, Totonacs erect an altar in their homes and place the things the dead people's spirits enjoyed while they were still alive—like food, tobacco, and rum. They believe that since they are spirits, they can only partake and enjoy the essence of these offerings. They also go to the graveyard to whitewash the gravestones and place flowers around them. There are always marigolds growing in their cultivated fields. On November 2, the Day of the Dead, people strip the petals from the marigolds and make a path of yellow petals from some dead relative's grave to their house to help their spirits find their way home.

On the Day of the Dead, Teyo's brother came to see Bessie. He told her how much Teyo had loved to hear her singing. He asked if she would please come to sing that song in Totonac to him that night when his spirit would return. Bessie wondered about the implications and decided not to go. She told him only live people could appreciate the message that Totonac song expressed. Later Bessie regretted her decision realizing there would also be people there who needed to hear that message.

While Bessie knew she had lost this one opportunity to use her voice for the Lord, she determined not to let it happen again. Using the technology of the day, she, with the help of Joy Ridderhof of Gospel Recordings, produced a series of records and then tape cassettes of her singing in Totonac. Later these songs would be played over the radio station run by Felipe Ramos. And in at least one case, Bessie's songs would be the catalyst for a man giving his life to the Lord.

*Elizabeth (Bessie) Dawson and Herman, married
August 16, 1941. They were married for fifty-seven
years.*

8

Making Friends

From the beginning Herman entered into the Totonac culture with empathy and acceptance. This absorption of all things Totonac later enabled him to produce meaningful New Testament translations in three different Totonac language variants. From his 1941 journal, Herman gives us a warm, intimate, nonjudgmental view of what life was like in Zapotitlán for himself and his new bride.

> The village then had about 3,000 inhabitants and was one of the principal market towns of the area. The town square, or plaza, was a bare space with the typical

Mexican kiosk in the center of the square. Market day was always on Sunday, and the town square would swell by the hundreds as people from surrounding villages came to buy and sell their wares. There were no stalls for the vendors, but the sellers arranged their vegetables, fruit and other foodstuffs, on the ground with surprising artistry. As always, market day was more than just a commercial venture. This was a time to socialize, to meet old friends, to make new ones, to exchange gossip and to have a good time.

It was on market days that Bessie and I came to talk and make friends with the people of Zapotitlán. The town had many stores mostly owned by *mestizos*, some of whom were longtime residents. Most of these merchants could also speak Totonac. The side streets that led into the plaza were full of the mules that had brought in the produce and merchandise for the market. American visitors called it the market parking lot.

Facing the plaza on one side was the town hall. Some of the town halls in that area had something ornate about them. And most of them also had something unfinished about them. The ornateness, as well as the unfinished part, had to do with the turn of the century when Porfirio Díaz was the president of Mexico. Díaz improved a number of prosperous areas like the Totonacapan (Spanish term for Totonac country). When the revolution came in 1910, many of the Totonacs joined the revolutionaries. The federal troops fought back and invaded the area and burned down some of the Indian villages such as Ixtepec and

Hueytlalpan and other towns close to Zapotitlan.

It was this revolution that opened the door for new families to come to Zapotitlán. One of these was Miguel Manzano's father who was one of the revolutionary generals. As a reward for his service, he was given land around Zapotitlán to cultivate. He was still living there in 1941 and invited Herman and Bessie to visit him and his wife in their home, which they did.

Another revolutionary Herman mentioned was Javier Luna. He was the political boss and second most prosperous man in town. Luna also owned the local sugarcane alcohol distillery. When he first met Herman, he said he wanted to know him better and invited Herman to visit him in his rum factory. One thing Javier Luna wanted Herman to know was that before the revolution he had been sent as a child to a Methodist missionary boarding school in the city of Tetela. However, during and after the revolution, all foreign missionaries were forced to leave Mexico.

> I often thought the Methodist missionaries must have had some influence on him since he was proud to show me his Spanish Bible. Javier also wanted to tell me he liked me, and liked what we were doing for the Totonacs and that he would protect us. In my talks with him, he justified his running a distillery that was producing the sugar cane alcohol that made many Indians alcoholics by explaining that he, more than others, was the right person to run a distillery. "Because when I see someone drinking too much, I have a rule in my store that such a person is not to be sold any more rum." He said he cared about alcoholics and tried to help anyone he saw drinking too much. His other justification was that if he, a good man, didn't make and sell the stuff, somebody worse than

he would be doing it. I often wondered if God would accept that kind of reasoning.

Another prosperous man Herman spoke about was the gentleman farmer, Don Javier. Herman noted that Don Javier hired mostly Totonacs from Zongozotla to work his lands. Since the men worked as day laborers, they were paid at the end of each working day. However, Don Javier had introduced the custom that with the day's pay went a *copita* (small cup or glass) of rum. Years later, when many people from Zongozotla became true followers of Christ, most quit drinking. When Don Javier saw the believers refuse their copita as part of their pay, he was impressed and told Herman he gave each one of them a little extra pay in place of the copita.

One Sunday, when Don Javier and Herman were chatting in the plaza, the subject came up of one's responsibility to God. Don Javier claimed there were many people who have gone astray whom God should not punish because their environment had made them what they were. Herman then related a story about twins, who were raised in the same environment, yet one became a bad person, and the other turned out well. Wasn't it because they both, of their own free will, chose to be what they became? Don Javier admitted that what Herman said was true.

> Don Javier then sighed and with a deep heartfelt longing said: "You know Don Pedro, people know me as a tough character because I don't let anyone take advantage of me. I have had to kill others to protect myself. But, I have the faith to believe that some day you are going to see me in heaven because of what Christ did for me on the cross." Wow! Only God knows our hearts. Only he knows if we are truly repentant or not. Who am I to judge him?

Years later, at sugarcane processing time, Don Javier died a terrible death while he was directing his workers to squeeze out the juice from the sugarcane.

> The process begins when a hole is dug out on a slope which is made in the shape of a chimney in which they build a fire. A large cauldron is then fit snugly over the fire with openings around it to let the heat pass up and around it. The sugarcane is thrust through the rollers that squeeze out the juice. The juice is then channeled down into the cauldron where it is boiled down to a fudge-like consistency. These sheet iron or copper cauldrons are as much as ten feet in diameter. During the rendering of the sugarcane, wood is continually fed to the fire to keep the juice boiling. When the juice has boiled down to where it will harden when cooled, the cauldron is lifted off the fire. The cauldrons have hoops on opposite sides in which to pass a long strong pole. With four men on each side of the pole, the cauldron is lifted out and placed aside to more easily spoon out the fudge into the earthenware molds to harden.
>
> It was just at this point as the workers were about to lift the cauldron that Don Javier tripped and his lower body slipped down into that hot fudge-like stuff. He was pulled out and taken home. A runner was immediately sent thirty miles to Zacapoaxtla to get a doctor. When the doctor arrived, there wasn't much he could do for him. Too much of his skin was affected and in a few days Don Javier died. I would like to see that old friend in heaven. Maybe this mishap made him truly open to receive God's gift of salvation in a sincerely repentant way.

The day after the bombing of Pearl Harbor on December 7, 1941, the newly-elected president of Mexico, Manuel Ávila Camacho (who had been the Secretary of War under President Cárdenas), enunciated an unmistakable, pro-Allied course of action. However, it wasn't until June 1, 1942, that Mexico formally declared war on Germany. This was after German submarines, operating in the Caribbean, torpedoed and sank two Mexican tankers—the *S.S. Potrero del Llano* on May 14, and the *Faja de Oro* on May 24.

Almost immediately a military officer was sent to each municipality and instituted that weekly (on Sundays) all the able-bodied men were to practice marching in their town squares. This was true even in the isolated areas of Mexico.

> Since I was part of the community, I wanted to show my solidarity behind Mexico's war effort and asked the captain who came to drill the men if I could join and march with the rest of the men from Zapotitlán. The captain said yes, and since I was the tallest man among them, he put me first in line. As for understanding all the technical marching orders and close order drill, I was just as clueless as some of the Totonacs who didn't know much Spanish. For a while it was quite a circus until we finally began to catch on. Then it was not only good exercise but a lot of fun.

In the spring of 1942, Herman and Bessie (pregnant with their first child) left Zapotitlán and went to the city of Puebla to be near a hospital for the baby's birth. At that time Tom Fountain, a new missionary with the Mexican Indian Mission, wanted to survey the area around Papantla, Veracruz. Papantla was a ceremonial and trade center around which the Lowland Totonac people lived on their ranches. His friend, Bob Dawson, also wanted to go with him. At the time, the only way to reach Papantla was by the main mule-trail route from

Zapotitlán. Aware that Herman knew the area, they asked him to be their guide to Zapotitlán. From there the three of them would make their way by foot to Papantla. Herman and Bessie had calculated the date when they believed the baby would be born, and Herman planned to return in plenty of time to get Bessie to the hospital.

> When we reached Zapotitlán we got Marcos Cortes to be our guide and off we went hiking to Papantla. It took us three days of walking to get there. By that time Tom was so exhausted he knew he couldn't make it back by foot with us to Zapotitlán. In those days there was plane service between Papantla and Poza Rica, so Tom flew there and then caught a bus to Mexico City. After he left, Bob, Marcos and I walked back to Zapotitlán and Puebla the same way we came.

> When we reached Bessie in Puebla, our son Robert was two weeks old! He had been born on June 27, 1942. What an ordeal that must have been for Bessie. The baby came at night. She had to wake up the Mexican friends with whom she was staying so they could take her to the hospital. I couldn't help but feel guilty for having left her at such a critical time.

> It was in the fall of 1942 that all those belonging to "The Townsend Group," as they then were called, gathered in Mexico City to attend our Mexico branch conference. Mr. William G. Nyman from Glendale, California also attended. He, with the aid of a lawyer and the Mexico Branch constitution the group used as a guide, to formulate the constitutions for Wycliffe Bible Translators as well as the Summer Institute of Linguistics. They did this in order for the two groups to become non-profit corporations in the State of

California. We, as founding members, now had to vote to accept both organizations and their by-laws. We also had to elect three more directors beside the incorporating directors who were: William Cameron Townsend, William G. Nyman (the group's Secretary-Treasurer), Kenneth Pike and Eugene Nida.

One reason for incorporating in the States was to change the name of "Camp Wycliffe" to "Summer Institute of Linguistics." This was more appropriate since the school's summer classes were now being held at the University of Oklahoma in Norman. We also needed the incorporation of Wycliffe Bible Translators as a sending organization. In this way our donors could receive tax deductible receipts for the financial support they sent to us. Previously the Pioneer Mission Agency Inc., a nonprofit organization in New Jersey, had graciously helped us by receiving and sending funds they received from our donors. Because there had been such a large influx of recruits that summer that took linguistic courses and then joined us in Mexico, the Pioneer Mission Agency said we had grown too large and they were no longer capable of receiving and sending our donations. We named our new organization after the fourteenth century English theologian, scholar and reformer John Wycliffe. Because Wycliffe believes in the primacy of scripture, he was the first scholar to seriously attempt the translation of the Bible into the English language.

After the formal incorporation of the two organizations, Mr. Townsend sent the following vision statement to the Pioneer Mission Agency: "The purpose of Wycliffe Bible Translators will be to forward, in every way possible, the project of putting the Word of God into all tribal [ethnic] tongues [languages] on earth in which it does not yet exist. Wycliffe will seek to assist all pioneer evangelical missionaries to receive specialized linguistic training, written helps and expert counsel for their task of reducing languages to writing, translating the scripture into them and teaching people to read the Word when it has been made available."

Just before Herman and Bessie left Zapotitlan to attend their conference in Mexico City, Manuel Arenas came to visit them and asked if he could go with them. He said he wanted to learn to speak better Spanish and even go to school, but Herman hesitated and said perhaps at a later time.

> While we were in Mexico City taking part in our conference, who should show up at our door step in Mexico City but Manuel Arenas. When we were about to leave Zapotitlán to come to our conference he asked to go with us to Mexico City to study so that he could get a good education in Spanish. I told him we didn't think that was a good idea. In the back of our minds we also did not want to lose him as our co-translator of the Totonac New Testament. But we underestimated Manuel's determination. How he ever found us I'll never know. Tearfully, he told us he had come to Mexico City so he could become a "somebody" with the prestige that a good education would give him. He said this was the only way he knew that would allow him to return and help his own people. Further, he said he had also broken ties with his father and without us there, he had no place in Zapotitlán to live.
>
> The first job Manuel found in Mexico City was in a saloon cleaning and mopping floors. Later he got a job

at our Institute with offices at the Kettle on Heroes street. (The "Kettle" was an old ornate house the Institute purchased from an elderly American lady who had used it as a sort of motel in which to put up tourists. She called it "Quetzalcoatl's Palace." We shortened that name to "the Kettle.")

The Kettle served as a haven for weary group members while they were in Mexico City. It also held our offices, storage space, dining room, meeting house and print shop. As more of us needed it as a place to stay, it became cramped quarters indeed. But we liked it so much that most of us who had to come to Mexico City would rather sleep there on the floor than go to a hotel. Its greatest asset was to give us a chance to have some close fellowship with each other.

For many years Manuel lived in Mexico City, went to night school, and educated himself. Along with his general education subjects, Manuel went to the International Business School where he took typing, bookkeeping, and shorthand. He also took an elective course in etiquette and proper dress habits. As an adult, Manuel was always a fastidious dresser.[29]

While Manuel was going to school, he was always willing to help us with translation. From time to time Manuel would return to Zapotitlán to continue translating with me. Later, after learning English, Manuel attended the University of Chicago and then later graduated from the Dallas Bible Institute. After that he learned enough German to get a three-year scholarship to study at the University of Nuremberg

29 Steven, *Manuel*, 57.

in Germany. Although he became quite erudite, the calling to be God's servant and translate the New Testament into his mother tongue never left him. To do this with the least interference possible, we took Manuel with us to the States for two of our furloughs. That also gave him an excellent opportunity to learn to speak English, and he took full advantage of it. Manuel's desire to learn to speak English was he believed the only avenue through which he would gain the recognition of his humanity, and that of his fellow Totonacs. This was a vision (rightly or wrongly) that captivated him all of his adult life. In 1985 part of this dream became a reality. In recognition of his outstanding leadership, both as a world citizen and among his own people, and for his role as an educator and co-translator of the Totonac New Testament, the John Calvin Theological Seminary in Mexico City conferred on Manuel Arenas the honorary degree of Doctor of Theology.

Manuel Arenas, principal co-translator of the Highland Totonac New Testament. Later he was the founder and director of the Totonac Cultural Center and Bible School.

9

Trying to Make Life Easier Doesn't Always Work

Manuel Arenas was in the prime of his youth when his burning curiosity about what life was like beyond his village of Zapotitlán took him to Mexico City. Manuel's birthday was never recorded, but Herman believed he was about fifteen or sixteen when one late afternoon he surprised them by knocking at their door in Mexico City. What further surprised Herman and Bessie was the way Manuel quickly embraced his new city lifestyle.

During his first years in Mexico City Manuel attended the Divino Salvador Presbyterian Church, just a block from the Zocalo (the central square or plaza in Mexico City). Manuel enjoyed the forms, liturgy and biblical teaching of a Protestant Presbyterian church service. But what he liked most were the hymns. These touched him deeply. He told me how on his way home from church, after hearing a new hymn he would think of a Totonac message whose words would fit the timing of the notes of the hymn. Within five years or so he had composed the Totonac words to go with some seventy-five hymn tunes. Although, years later, when other Totonacs had also composed their share of new hymns in Totonac, the oldies that Manuel made in the forties are the ones the Totonacs still liked to sing the most.

In 1946, Joy Ridderhof from Gospel Recordings came to Mexico with recording equipment to produce gospel Victrola records in the Indian languages. She asked Manuel to put in writing short gospel messages in Totonac that she could record. Manuel would then read them as Joy recorded them. She then recorded Bessie as she sang several of Manuel's hymns in Totonac. Later Joy processed this material in her Los Angeles studios.

In 1949, Bessie and I went to Los Angeles to record more of Bessie's singing in Totonac, this time with an accompaniment. They recorded her singing some of the Totonac hymns as duets with herself. These were the recordings the Indians liked most. The technology behind these recordings was always puzzlement to the Totonacs. We had enough material to fill nine double-sided Victrola records. A hundred copies of each were made for us. As the years went by, all of these were bought and soon worn out by Totonac listeners. Fortunately some of them were later copied to cassette tapes.

The Aschmanns were, like the early SIL workers, unique to their time. In order for translators working in isolated areas to remain connected to the broader society, the Mexico Branch directorate ruled workers should return to Mexico City every six months for a period of R & R. But Herman and Bessie like many others—that included Marianna Slocum and Florence Gerdel working among the Tzeltal, Paul and Ellen Carlson among the Tarahumaras, and Phil and Mary Bear among the Lacandón—either forgot or ignored the rule.

During our early years we spent many months at a time living with the Totonacs. We were supposed to come out to Mexico City every six months, but we were often out there as long as nine months at a time. There was always something we badly wanted to keep doing.

When we did come out it was mostly because Bessie was about to have another baby. On one such trip to Mexico City Bessie, who was seven months pregnant and too big with child to be able to straddle the saddle, was sitting sidesaddle. We had just reached the outskirts of Zacapoaxtla when a truck came roaring down the road toward where we were coming with the animals. This startled Bessie's horse and it swung around and took off in a different direction. Before Bessie knew what was happening she began sliding down the side of the horse with both of her feet high in the air. Just as she was about to fall off she somehow got a firmer grip on the saddle horn. Fortunately the truck stopped, and the three Mexican men were able to grab the horse and lift

Bessie back up onto the saddle. They were most apologetic that such a thing should have happened.

In 1943 Bessie (who was an Australian citizen) flew with her son Rob to Los Angeles to stay with her parents to finally fulfill her five years of residence and be sworn in as a naturalized U.S. citizen. Meanwhile, Herman returned to Zapotitlán to live a bachelor's life among the Totonacs.

> One evening when I was by myself, I had a surprise visit from Manuel Arenas, George Cowan,[30] Jack Wyrtzen and Glen Wagner, a hulk of a man who was a youth evangelist. Glen was a former football player with Red Grange in I think Illinois.[31] They had come to Mexico to spend a few days with me just to see how a translator lived and worked among an ethnic group.

> The twelve-hour hike from Zacapoaxtla must have been quite an experience for Jack and Glen. They really weren't in good physical shape to hike that long up and down trail by foot. It was also quite an experience for me to get food prepared for them to eat and to house them. One day Jack asked me to invite some of the Totonac boys to come to our house so he could witness to them. With Manuel's help I was able to gather in a few fellows to come and listen. Even with the two of us acting as interpreters I'm afraid we didn't do too well in converting his English message into meaningful Totonac.

Many years after this visit with Herman, George Cowan, who was then president emeritus of Wycliffe Bible Translators International,

---

30 George Cowan would later become the director of the Mexico Branch.
31 Just for clarification, Jack Wyrtzen and Glen Wagner were visitors and not officially connected with Wycliffe or SIL.

wrote me a three-page letter to fill in details of that trip missing from Herman's notes.

> With Manuel as our guide, and when public transportation ended, we arrived at the trail head and tried to secure horses to take us up the long trail to Herman's village. It was here we ran into a problem. Nobody wanted to rent their horses to us. The problem was Glen. When the owners of the horses saw this huge man who weighed over 250 pounds they said he was too heavy for their horses. But finally when we promised to trade off horses en-route, so no one horse had to carry him all the way, one owner agreed.
>
> Jack Wyrtzen had been in the cavalry in military service and was used to riding. But Glen Wagner was a different story. Getting him off one horse and remounted on another was quite an operation. Because of his weight we had to find a big rock for him to stand on in order to get him up into the saddle. Once I thought he was going to heave himself clear over the horse and land on the ground on other side. It was a long hard trip over a narrow slippery muddy trail. The hoofs of the previous animals had left deep holes filled with water that squirted up all over Manuel and me as we walked along behind the animals. When we finally arrived after dark, we were covered with mud from head to foot. When I took off my trousers for the night they had dried enough so they stood up by themselves.
>
> On Saturday night Jack asked Herman to have a "Saturday night rally." Earlier, thinking of his large Saturday programs in Madison Square Garden, Jack wrote a telegram greeting from Totonac country to be

read at the rally. Herman found a Totonac man who was willing to walk all night to take the message to the telegraph office in the lowlands. At Herman's request Manuel rounded up three or four young boys, and with the visitors as onlookers, with Herman translating as best he knew how (he was still learning the language), Jack preached an evangelistic sermon.[32]

George Cowan reminded me that while Herman's facility in Totonac was limited, the Lord was in Jack's message. Manuel later said it was after hearing that message that he gave his heart to the Lord. Many years later, Manuel was to give his testimony at Jack Wyrtzen's famous Madison Square Garden rally. During the summer of 1944, SIL held their linguistic summer school at Bacone College, a school for Indian children in Muskogee, Oklahoma. At the conclusion of the summer courses, Bessie and Rob joined Herman. From there they traveled to Port Chester, New York, to visit Herman's mother. Bessie had never met her or any of Herman's old hometown friends. On that trip Herman's mother bought him another car. It was in this car that Herman and Bessie nearly lost their lives. George Cowan ended his three-page letter with the following story:

> We were just terminating our weekly evening prayer meeting in our Mexico City headquarters when we received a phone call from Bessie [Aschmann]. She and Herman were returning to Mexico City by car when suddenly out of the dark a drunken man on horseback appeared on the road in front of them and they crashed into him. The horse and man ended up over the engine of the car and the man was killed. A passing car had picked up Bessie and took her to where

---

32 This was a one-time event as a courtesy to an instant visitor. It is against SIL protocol for its members to enter into formal, church-related leadership. The policy of SIL is for the local church to be self-supporting, with preaching and leadership roles in the hands of national people.

she [could] call us. The police had taken Herman and the car but she didn't know where. She was able to tell us more or less where they were on the highway. Immediately I and one of our other members jumped into his car and drove to the nearest area where the accident happened. We checked with the highway patrol to see if they knew where Herman might be, but they didn't know.

According to Mexican custom we knew Herman would probably be in jail. So in the middle of the night we started hunting for him, but to our dismay no one seemed to know anything about the accident or where Herman was. We learned later no one wants to get involved so they plead ignorance. After visiting several villages around the area we gave up the search for the night but resumed the search early the next morning. Finally, we found Herman sitting in the town plaza chatting happily with some of the local people. He told us he'd been put in jail but the local official with whom he had talked to ended up inviting him to his home where he got some sleep in a comfortable bed.

Herman was freed and our Mexican group insurance handled the case with no criminal charges against him. When Herman learned the family had lost its breadwinner and received no financial payment or help, he got in touch with the family and gave them a gift of money. For some time afterward I learned he gave them further financial help from his own limited income.

On June 10, 1945, the Aschmanns' second son, Timothy, was born in the American Hospital in Mexico City. Then on November 2, 1946, their daughter, Rachel Ellen, was also born in that same hospital.

> Try to imagine watching our little troop winding its way for ten or twelve hours down that usually muddy trail from Zacapoaxtla to Zapotitlán! The Totonacs carried their loads on their backs tied to a tumpline which rested on their foreheads. When our children were still babies we tucked each child down in Indian carrying baskets called *huacales* with a cloth over them to shade them from the sun. Then when the children were two or three years old and could sit up, we used a bigger padded wooden crate to put them in. I nailed a foot rest at the bottom so that their legs wouldn't be dangling. To the children this was fun and the up-and-down motion of the carrier worked like magic to put them to sleep as they went along.
>
> It rained a lot in those jungle mountains and it was very uncomfortable if, while traveling, we got caught in a downpour. We used a poncho for raincoats. This was a large square rubberized piece of canvas with a slit in the middle for the head to go through. Sometimes we had one of the children sit on the horse behind or in front of us. We tried not to do that often as it was dangerous. We found that out once when it was raining and the trail was exceptionally muddy. In some places the mud puddles on the trail were deep enough for the water to come up to the horse's belly as they waded through. Once we wanted Rob and Tim to get a change from riding in their boxes so Bessie had one of them sit in front of her and the other one sat behind her on her horse. As her horse sloshed through one of the mud holes, its front legs got stuck in the soft

mud. Suddenly the horse gave a jump as it struggled to free itself, and off went the three of them into the air to land in the underbrush at the side of the road. No one was hurt but it taught us to never do that again.

Once during the fifties while the Aschmanns were living in Mexico City, Herman took the four older children for a brief visit to their new home in Nanacatlan[33] (Bessie wasn't feeling well and stayed home). When the children and Herman arrived in Nanacatlan they went right to their big house by the pasture. One of Herman's first duties was to light the kerosene refrigerator. Unthinkingly he put a glass bottle partially full of gasoline on top of the refrigerator and forgot about it. Rob was in the kitchen holding a machete in his hand.

For reasons unknown, Rob rushed out of the kitchen waving the machete. As he ran, he knocked over the bottle full of gasoline, which ran down the back of the refrigerator. When it reached the lighted wick in the back of the refrigerator, it burst into flames. Herman immediately grabbed the cracked bottle and flung it on to the cobblestone floor of the big middle room where it broke into many pieces. Fortunately Herman was able to put out the fire surrounding the refrigerator, but he couldn't quench the burning gasoline in the other room. He just let it burn itself out. Said Herman, "After that our precious kerosene refrigerator never worked again. What a loss that was!"

It was a loss not only for its lack of utility, but also for the Herculean effort it took to get the refrigerator transported over the rugged, steep mountain trails.

> The refrigerator had two parts to it, the back and working parts which weighed 200 pounds. There was the shell which weighed slightly less but was bulky. In order to get it to Zapotitlán, we hired a number

---

33 Herman and Bessie lived in Zapotitlán from 1941–1948. After a furlough (1948–1949), they moved to the village of Nanacatlan. See Chapter 10 for a fuller explanation of why they moved.

of strong professional carriers. These were men who could carry heavy loads on their backs for long distances. To make it easier for the carriers I took the refrigerator apart into its two parts. We then placed each part on stretchers. After two of the carriers tied their tumplines to it, fore and aft, they took off with the load equally distributed on their backs as well as on their foreheads. It took the four of them two days to make it from Zacapoaxtla to Zapotitlán. Then it took just a half a day to get it up to Nanacatlan.

We also brought in a gasoline-run electric light plant as well as an electric clothes washing machine. At first electric lights were somewhat of a nuisance since they brought in too many visitors at night. However, when the curiosity wore off, the visitors quickly dwindled. In the daytime our house was usually full with visiting Totonacs. Some came out of curiosity; others found it a good place to pass the time away. We got used to having them around and just went about our business as if they weren't there.

Herman's ideas for making living easier for the family didn't always turn out as planned. One of his projects was to dig a well in his backyard. But this proved unsanitary as the only water to fill the well was surface water that rose and fell according to the rainfall.

That was easy to see when we had the first good rainstorm and the well filled up almost to the surface of the ground. Then in a few days the level had gone down to ten yards below ground level. The ground in front of the house was the beginning of a slope that went up abruptly a thousand feet to the top of the mountain. I had one of the Totonac men dig us a well a ways up the slope. I planned to bring the water by gravity down to the house via plastic piping. The result was a beautiful well that soon filled with water. Then much to our dismay, with the next storm, the well caved in and I could see no way to repair it. The ground washed and caved in too easily.

Herman's son Dan also remembers the construction of the backyard well.

It was the first well in the village and the Totonacs were not happy with the idea. The Totonac people believed the spirits of the springs would get upset if you created your own source of water. Many people thought we would get sick or die because of what we were doing.

Dan had other memories of life in the village and related the following story:

One night when my brother Rick and I were getting ready for bed, I accidentally knocked over the kerosene lamp. When it broke it started a big fire in the middle of the bedroom. When I called my mom, she came in and calmly threw a heavy army blanket over the flame and it went out. She then told us to finish getting ready for bed, and walked out with the scorched blanket. She was one tough woman.

But by far Dan's fondest memories of living among the Totonacs as a young child had to do with how much freedom he had.

When I was very young, I was something of a curiosity in the village. No one then had seen blond hair, much less blue eyes. They would ask me if my eyes hurt. Often someone would touch or feel my hair. This let me get away with a lot of stuff. I loved to hang out in the main store in town because there was a big candy jar on the counter. I would go in and sit on the counter and ask for a piece of candy. Since I was somewhat of an ornament for the store, the proprietor would feed my addiction as long as I sat on the counter and watched the Totonacs come and go in the store. And, oh yes, like Tom Sawyer, I always went barefoot with my Indian friends.

Herman's great gift as a translator was his love for the Totonac people, their language, and culture.

10

Accidents Will Happen

In the early 1940s, Herman had to answer two basic translation questions before he began his translation. One, did he understand the Totonac language well enough for his translation to communicate the same meaning as the original? Two, would the translation communicate as clearly and as idiomatically as the original did? In order to achieve these goals Herman needed to immerse himself in the Totonac language. The problem was that while Herman and Bessie lived in Zapotitlán, most of the people were Spanish speakers who couldn't or wouldn't speak to them in Totonac.

To make the best use of their language-learning time, Herman decided they needed to move to a village where everyone would speak to them in Totonac. For years Herman had looked for a town that had a house big enough to accommodate his growing family. One of the towns he passed through on his way to various other towns was the little village of Nanacatlan (population 500), a half hour's walk from Zapotitlán. Each time Herman passed through Nanacatlan, Indalecio Rodriguez, who owned the only store in town, would invite him to stop and talk. The more Herman talked to Indalecio, the more he realized Nanacatlan was the ideal place for him to gain a deeper insight into the Highland Totonac language. Herman bought a plot from Indalecio and had a carpenter build him a house. However, the house turned out to be one room of rough boards with no windows.

> I knew with our growing family we would have a problem living in such cramped quarters. But at the time, that was all we could afford. Then, to my surprise, Indalecio offered to rent us his large stone house on the edge of town that had been built by his grandfather. After his grandfather died, it stood vacant for many years.

Herman accepted Indalecio's kind offer, and after selling his house he and Bessie moved into the stone house. And what a house it was. In every way it was the complete opposite of Herman and Bessie's rough-board house. The walls of the stone house were sixteen inches thick. The floor was cobblestone. There was no ceiling except for a loft which covered half of the kitchen. The windows were big—three feet by six feet—with shutters but no windowpanes. The front and back doors were huge—five feet by eight feet. The kitchen fireplace that served as their cooking corner was a raised masonry hearth. Above it was a funnel-like chimney made of boards that went up into the loft and served to take away the smoke. There was a pasture that surrounded the house on three sides. Just 200 yards away in the pasture was a spring where the townspeople went for potable water. In front of the house was a large bougainvillea bush. Its vine-like branches formed a canopy that stretched across the street and ended up resting on the roof of the stone house. Because Indalecio's house had been built on the site of an ancient cemetery, no one had wanted to live in it. The new cemetery was situated on top of a hill on the other side of the pasture. One of the unexpected features of the house was that it was built on the side of the main trail route that went down to Zapotitlán. This gave Herman ample opportunity to hear and speak Totonac with people coming and going on the trail. Herman recalled that the move to Nanacatlan went more smoothly than he expected. Further, Indalecio told Herman and Bessie they could make any innovations they cared to. The first thing Herman did was to bring in a flush toilet from Mexico City and to dig a covered septic tank in the backyard.

Although the spring where they had to go for potable water was 200 yards from the house, it proved no problem for the two girls who helped Bessie in the kitchen. They could carry hundreds of gallons of water to the house in earthenware jars on their heads. Rather than being a burden, Herman said this was something the girls enjoyed doing. Herman installed a 100-gallon metal barrel in the loft over the kitchen, where the girls emptied their jars of water. From there he ran pipes into the kitchen as well as the bathroom at the back of the house. One of Herman's few hobbies was his love of horticulture. He planted flowers, citrus fruit trees, and a vegetable garden.

> Our backyard became our vegetable garden. Here again
> we found that in that jungle climate certain things grew
> profusely while others were hopeless. Vegetables like
> lettuce and cabbage were eaten up voraciously by the
> bugs. I planted some grapefruit seeds. When the seed-
> lings were big enough I grafted some seedless navel

> orange buds to them. That was a great success. Another success was with the chayote vines along the backyard fence that produced abundantly. You could cook the fruit like you would potatoes. The succulent tips of the vines were also a delicious green vegetable. The tubers were also tasty. The two vines I planted bore so profusely we had enough to store the tubers in the loft over the kitchen. They kept well for many months.

Herman also recalled how well their three children—Rob, Tim, and Rachel—adapted to the move to Nanacatlan.

> The children fit in well with the many Totonac children that came around. Once Tim told us how he and some other boys found a wild bees' nest in the hollow of a tree. They smoked out the bees and went in to pull out the combs that contained the bee larvae. They started a fire and roasted the larvae in a frying pan and ate them. We didn't much like this especially when Tim said that he had done this with them more than once. We told him it wasn't a good idea to do that anymore. But really, now, is there anything wrong in eating fried bees' larvae or was it just the unusual we were afraid of?

One of the unspoken tensions for anyone living with children in an isolated village is the ever-present concern of what to do in a medical emergency. Herman and Bessie were keenly aware that with children accidents were bound to happen. In his memoirs, under the heading, "Accidents Happen," Herman related three events that came close to the unthinkable.

> One day Rob was in the pasture trying to catch our donkey when the donkey kicked him in the forehead. I thank God Rob was wearing his hat because it buffered

the blow. The donkey's hoof just barely made it to his head just above where the hat started. Otherwise the blow might have killed him. When we sold the donkey, it promptly took a bite out of the new owner's hand. There is nothing more unpredictable than a donkey!

On yet another occasion Bessie and Rachel had gone with the village women to the big river. While Rachel was walking along the river's edge, she slipped on some wet rocks, fell into the river and was carried away by the swift current. Bessie immediately jumped in and was able to grab Rachel. But the force of river continued to carry them both downstream at a fast pace. Finally after much struggling to keep their heads above water, Bessie found a good footing and dragged herself and Rachel out of the water visibly shaken but thankful to God they were alive. The Totonac women were devastated when they saw what was happening. They were afraid they might be blamed if Bessie or Rachel had drowned.

Once we tied three 40-gallon empty gasoline drums to the saddle of our donkey for a trip to Zapotitlán. We then sat Rachel on the rump of the donkey and told her to hold on as we went down the trail together. When the donkey started to trot, the drums hit against each other and made a noise that frightened it. Before we knew what was happening, the donkey took off at full gallop with poor Rachel holding on for dear life. Fortunately we were able to catch up with them and rescue her.

While Herman concentrated mostly on linguistics and the study of the Totonac language, Bessie made a major contribution to the Totonac community through her medical work. With only a year of nurse's training, she found herself, by default, to be the only medical provider in the area.

> Bessie patched up people who were injured in accidents or in drunken fights with machetes. She once had to treat a man who had gone fishing with dynamite and neglected to release the dynamite stick in time after having lit the fuse. He had lost part of his arm and an eye. Bessie did what she could for him, and praises God he lived.
>
> Bessie's Physicians Desk Reference (PDR) became a second bible to her as she referenced it to treat hundreds of cases of intestinal problems and infections of various kinds. However, in many cases, the problems she treated were not listed in the PDR. While the people came to her for their cuts, bruises and infections she was at first never asked to help the women when they were in labor.
>
> The midwives and shaman were the ones usually called in to help on those occasions. Generally they were quite good at it. The breakthrough for Bessie came one day when in desperation someone came to Bessie for help with a woman who had been in labor a long time and was now too weak to bring forth her child. Fortunately Bessie had some digitalis and gave the girl a shot which gave her the strength to give birth to her child. After this, others began to call on her to help with those in labor but only when it was a case too hard for the midwives to handle.

Besides her medical work, Bessie also had a ministry with several of the young Totonac girls who helped with kitchen and household duties.

Lola, Leonila, Patsi, and Delfina were some of the girls that came from time to time to help Bessie. These girls were helpful in going for water, patting out tortillas, cooking certain meals, and washing clothes. Besides being good companions for Bessie, they afforded Bessie and me good practice in Totonac. One day, one of these girls, I can't remember which one, was in the kitchen patting out and cooking tortillas when in came a young man who, without a word, took her by the hand and marched out of the house with her. To our surprise and astonishment the girl showed no resistance. When we asked Delfina what was going on, she said the fellow was eloping with her.

I immediately caught up with them and told the young man he shouldn't be doing such a thing. Whereupon he looked me in the eye and said, "Look you don't know our customs. Just leave us alone." When I inquired further about this unusual behavior I was told the young man was justified in doing this because he may not have had the fifty pesos to buy the marriage license. I never did learn what town he took her to. But years later they were back in town living happily with each other. Could it be that marriage is more a commitment than a piece of paper? Those two must have believed that because they turned out to be fully committed to each other for life, like God wants all married couples to be.

Bessie was frequently asked to visit someone who might need her medical help. But sometimes the request for a visit had nothing to do with the medicine she was trained to offer.

One day when Bessie went to the woman's house who

had asked for her help, she discovered the mother of the family wanted her to pray for her dead son. Apparently the boy had gone with another boy to the big river perhaps to bathe or go fishing. Somehow her son had fallen in the river and drowned. As Bessie tried to console her, it became apparent that what the mother really wanted was for Bessie to pray that something bad should happen to her son's companion.

The mother thought the boy in some way must have been to blame for her son's death. Rather than pray for some evil to befall the boy, Bessie prayed instead that God would take away such evil thoughts from the mind of this poor woman. The mother must have thought Bessie's prayers had the same power as a shaman's ritual when he passed a curse on someone. We hope that Bessie's prayer produced results, but not the kind that Totonac woman desired.

*Felipe Ramos, pastor, radio voice of the Totonac Cultural Hour,
Dean of the Totonac Bible School and co-translator
with Herman on the Totonac New Testaments.*

11

New Helpers

Like the birth and growth of the New Testament church in Acts, the
Totonac church was full of improbabilities and amazing examples of
faith in action. For example, when a young man named Isidro discovered the translated Totonac scriptures had an answer to the longing
of his heart, he invited his relatives to come to his home to read and
study the translated Gospel of Mark. Later he did the same as other
books were translated.

By this time, Manuel Arenas had translated the words
for a number of hymns into Totonac that the little

group had learned by heart and loved to sing. On Sundays, Bessie and I with other believers would go up to Zongozotla to help them. There were always a goodly number of other believers from the surrounding villages who gathered together in Zapotitlán on Sundays. Not only Totonacs but Aztecs from Huitzilan would attend as well. Vicente Cortes, who spoke Aztec in addition to his mother tongue Totonac, would teach them. Soon the number of believers in Zongozotla had multiplied into the hundreds and it was then they built a concrete roofed church that could seat five hundred. Later they had to expand the walls of their church so that it now holds over a thousand people.

Herman noted in his memoirs that Zongozotla, a town of some four thousand, was one of the most pitiable Totonac villages in the area. Alcoholism was rampant, and that meant poverty. But with thanks to God, Herman said the first believers became the catalysts that changed an entire community.

Zongozotla is coffee country. When the believers stopped drinking alcohol they had extra cash that allowed them to prosper materially as well as spiritually. Even those who did not believe or attend the church were affected by the new life style of the believers when they saw their children were better dressed and were healthier than those who were addicted to alcohol. Over time this positive influence of the first believers dramatically changed the drunken, backward character of the whole town. It is now one of the most progressive towns in the area.

Eventually Miguel Cano, Isidro's son, became the pastor of the church in Zongozotla. Isidro had sent him to study at the Mexican Indian Mission's Bible school in Tamazunchale. Miguel proved to be an excellent preacher, and the church grew under his leadership. After forty years as their leader, Miguel became blind, but that did not stop him from preaching. When Miguel realized he could no longer be the preaching pastor of the church, he began recording his messages in Totonac onto cassette tapes. Now even those who do not believe or attend the church are being reached by his tapes.

One of the other improbabilities of God working through cassette tapes happened when Bessie—with her beautiful, clear, bell-like voice—recorded hymns in Totonac. One day Herman received a phone call from Jose Jimenez, a mechanical engineer, who was teaching in a school in Tijuana. He was a Totonac man formally from the city of Papantla, where Herman would one day do a translation of the Papantla Totonac New Testament.

At first Jose said he just wanted to talk. But then he wanted to know if Herman had any more of those cassettes in Highland Totonac where Bessie sang about God's love. He said his mother had died and he was homesick for a reminder from back home. He then told Herman something he had never told him before: "Years ago, while I was listening to Bessie's beautiful voice sing those wonderful hymns in the Highland dialect of Totonac, I just couldn't resist any longer and turned my life over to Christ."

Here was this sophisticated man telling Herman that somewhere way back in time, while still a teenager living on the outskirts of Papantla, God met his heartfelt need for forgiveness as he listened to Bessie sing the good news of the gospel in the Totonac language. It was the salvation message in song that touched his heartstrings, even though it was in a different dialect!

In the early 1940s, Vicente Cortes led many fellow Totonacs to Christ. So many that Herman felt led to go to Tamazunchale, where Dr. John

Dale had his Bible school, to ask if he could send someone to Zapotitlán to organize the believers in the surrounding villages. Herman wanted to connect them with a fellowship of Totonac churches called "La Union de Iglesias." After Herman and Bessie moved to Nanacatlán, Dr. Dale sent Loren and Betty Edigar to live in Zapotitlán. Herman noted that while the Edigars didn't speak Totonac, there were always Spanish speakers to help them. Herman said they did a good job of getting the Totonac believers to choose elders in the towns where there were enough believers to form a congregation.

> They sent Mario Luis, the pastor in Zapotitlán, and Miguel Cano from Zongozotla, to get Bible school training at the Bible school in Tamazunchale. Then along came Ricardo Garcia an evangelist, to reach the mestizos in Zapotitlán. Of all these assorted helpers, the one to whom those early believers owed the most was Vicente Cortes, the Totonac evangelist and the very first Totonac believer.

Herman was fond of telling the story about the tallest man in Nanacatlan, who came to see him early one morning.

> It was sometime in the early 1950s that Severo Ramo came to see me. When he greeted me that early morning, he had a smile from ear to ear. He came just to tell me he had decided to follow Christ. He said that Mariano Luna had persuaded him to become a believer.

Severo was the father of Felipe Ramos, who with Mariano served as elders when an organized church had its beginning in Nanacatlan. Mariano built a little, thatch-roofed chapel beside his house. That is where they met for services with the believers for most of the years Herman and Bessie lived in Nanacatlan. As the years passed, Herman noticed that most that came to the services in the little chapel were related. However, that all changed when Carlos Acosta, another of Dr. Dale's evangelists, came to visit the Aschmanns.

> There were so many who wanted to hear what the evangelists had to say that we opened our home to accommodate them. This brought in many people who weren't related to Mariano or Severo. After Carlos Acosta left, we had a problem since everyone wanted to keep coming to our house to hold services.

It was during one of the services in Herman's house that Felipe Ramos began taking the children aside to teach them separately. He felt so comfortable and fulfilled while doing this, he decided to take a year's study at the Bible school in Tamazunchale. To further his education, Felipe studied for another year at the Central American Seminary in the city of Puebla. After this, he returned to become the pastor of the church in Nanacatlan. Under his leadership the believers built a new church building. The cooperation of all those interested in its building broke up the clan spirit and made everyone feel more comfortable when they met together.

But all was not well with Felipe's health. Later in 1960, Herman suspected that Felipe's constant coughing was more than just a cold. When Herman took him to see a doctor in Mexico City, Felipe was diagnosed as having tuberculosis. Thankfully Herman was able to admit him into the TB hospital just a few blocks away from SIL's new headquarters in Tlalpan.[34] After two years of treatment, Felipe was pronounced cured and returned home to continue as the pastor of the Nanacatlan church. Later he went to La Union[35] to help Manuel Arenas build classes at his Bible school. After Manuel died,[36] Felipe returned to Nanacatlan, where he is now ministering to his people as

---

34 Tlalpan was a district, or *colonia*, on the outskirts of Mexico City.
35 La Union is the village and location of the church La Union del Iglesias and where Manuel Arenas had his Bible School.
36 Manuel Arenas died on May 27, 1992. See Appendix, "Reflections on the Death of a Friend."

well as teaching some of the young Totonac men of the area who also want to become pastors and establish new churches in the surrounding villages.

During the long, hot summer of 1948 and into 1949, much of the world's attention was focused on the Soviet blockade of West Berlin. One of the enduring photos of that summer was of American C-54s ferrying goods to a beleaguered city. This was high drama. But there was another kind of life-giving drama taking place. After almost seven nonstop years of intense, rustic tribal living, Herman and Bessie took a much-needed furlough in Norman, Oklahoma. This was a strategic move since Bessie began homeschooling their son Rob in first grade using the Calvert correspondence program. And Herman had come to Norman with Manual Arenas to concentrate on Bible translation.

> We wanted to complete the first draft of the Highland Totonac New Testament. Alas, we didn't quite make it. It was only later in 1950 when we again took Manuel with us to Sulphur Springs, Arkansas that we finally finished translating the entire first draft. Some of it was ready for printing. Other portions of it still had to be checked and improved. We did that from time to time with Manuel as well as with other Totonacs in Nanacatlan.

When they had finished the first draft of the New Testament in 1950, Herman wanted to give Manuel a gift for all the years he had worked with him. Up to that time Manuel had refused to take any pay for his work. This time, however, Manuel took Herman's gift of two hundred dollars. He used the money to travel by bus to Los Angeles to see Joy Ridderhof in her Gospel Recordings studios. There he composed the words for a few more Totonac hymns. Joy had him sing them while she recorded them, along with more of his short messages. With this collection of singing and readings, he had produced a new Victrola record for his Totonac people. While the summer of 1950 was notable for the completion of the first draft of the Totonac New Testament, this was almost overshadowed by the near death of Aschmann's daughter Rachel on their way to Sulphur Springs:

> We were on our way to Sulphur Springs, Arkansas where we would spend a furlough year. Our car was an old Dodge with the back seat doors opening out backwards. We happened to take off with the right back door not completely latched. Rachel, seeing the door on her side was ajar, opened it thinking to slam it shut. Instead, the force of wind caught the door and swung it completely open. Rachel was still holding onto the door handle and flew out of the car. Her outstretched body rolled down a culvert by the side of the road. When I realized what had happened, I felt sure she must have been killed. I stopped the car. Rob got out, picked her up and we rushed her to a clinic in Noel just a few miles away.
>
> When the doctor examined her, he discovered some wounds that had to be stitched, but there were no broken bones. After an overnight hospital stay, Rachel was well enough the next morning for us to take her home with thanks to God for sparing her life.

Totonac New Testament translated by Herman Aschmann.

12

The Book That Smacked of the Truth

It happened every Sunday evening for as many years as the Mexico Branch used the Kettle as their office headquarters and limited living quarters. On that night, members and friends gathered for an informal time to sing hymns, hear a devotional speaker, and listen to firsthand reports from translators and others who had recently returned from their village locations. For many, this was a time of warm fellowship and spiritual refreshment. One Sunday night in 1954, a report that made everyone stand up and cheer (if not physically, then most certainly inwardly) came from Herman Aschmann.

This week I finally gave the translation of the Highland Totonac to Allen Farson[37] to print for the American Bible Society. This simple act means that twelve years of hard work is now over. We owe so much to Manuel Arenas for his total commitment in producing the New Testament with us.

From his journal Herman recalled the following incident:

At that time we were living at our headquarters in Mexico City. On Sunday evening we gathered in the *sala*[38] for a time of reports and fellowship. When I reported I had given the Highland Totonac New Testament to be printed, Uncle Cam stood to congratulate me. He said: "When I first met and talked to Herman in 1938, I wondered about him. He just didn't seem to me to have much going for him. Was I ever wrong! Just think, here he is the third person in Wycliffe to produce a translation of the New Testament in an Indian language." Thanks Uncle Cam. Coming from you that meant a lot.

The years 1954 through 1964 were for Herman, Bessie, and the family a mixture of great joy and searing pain. Turning in the Highland New Testament for printing was, of course, a moment of great joy as was the birth of Richard, their sixth child, on June 11, 1955. After Richard was born, Herman was asked by the Mexico Branch directorate to assume the important position of "Government Man."

My job was to see that everyone's visas and immigration

---

37 Allen Farson with his brother Ken were longtime Wycliffe friends and colleagues. For a short time, Allen was a Wycliffe member. Both brothers ran printing establishments. One in Cuernavaca Mexico, and the other in Glendale, California, called The Church Press. They were both dedicated to printing Christian materials.
38 Spanish for "living room."

permits were renewed and kept in order. I had to constantly type requests for renewals and went daily to the government offices for one request or another. At first I felt I was the least qualified for such a job. But after a while I actually liked it. I saw how even bureaucrats and people in high places were really just ordinary people. There may also be something about me that must make me look like I'm naïve and helpless. This was an asset. It made those who helped me feel good in doing so. However, that sometimes meant endless waiting and going from office to office until I finally got results. It also helped to keep me humble. I served off and on as Government Man for over ten years, and made a few good Mexican friends in the process.

During some of the years that Herman served as the Government Man, he, Bessie, and the children lived in Mexico City. Dr. Ben Elson, the director of the Mexico Branch, with his wife Adelle, lived in an apartment next to the Aschmanns. When I asked Ben and Adelle what they remembered about Herman, they said:

One of Herman's outstanding characteristics was his patience and gentle personality. Once when Bessie was sick they lived next door to us. There were three apartments, each with three rooms; the outer room or first room as you entered was a small *sala*. That's where Herman and Manuel were translating. Herman's five children would be running in and out as they played in the patio. But mostly it seemed they liked to play in the small room where Herman and Manuel worked. They would climb on the back of Herman's chair and sit on Manuel's lap while others played on the floor. It was noisy and how the two men could concentrate was a miracle to all of us who passed by the room. The door was always open and we could observe how patient and gentle Herman was with his children, and with Bessie.

As an afterword, Ben said Herman was one of the finest Government Men ever to hold the office. The Mexican officials he worked with thought very highly of him.

One of the first seasons of frightening pain for Herman and Bessie occurred in January 1958 while Bessie was being operated on for an ovarian infection. Inexplicably, her heart stopped during the operation. To start Bessie's heart pumping again, the doctor had to keep pounding on her chest. The doctor finally arrested the problem and finished the operation. When Bessie came to, she wondered why her chest hurt so much. Herman told her how near death she had come and how concerned he and the family were that she might have further serious heart problems.

Since Bessie's heart was now in question and they were assigned long-term to live in Mexico City, they brought their four older children back from the children's home in Sulphur Springs and from Briercrest Academy in Caronport, Saskatchewan, Canada, to live with them and go to school in Mexico City. Herman noted it would have been a tight squeeze for their family of eight to live at the Kettle. But a freestanding house was too expensive for their budget. They solved their problem by renting the lower floor of a house about five miles from the Kettle, from a widow landlady who lived upstairs.

> Our four older children attended school at the Pan American Workshop nearby. We also had our faithful little Totonac helper Patsi to assist Bessie with the housework. She slept in the small garage that stood next to the house.

In 1959, four years after Herman gave the Highland Totonac New

Testament to Allen Farson for printing, a handsome, red-covered Totonac New Testament came off the press ready for distribution. This was an occasion for a great celebration, and Miguel Cano, the pastor of the church in Zongozotla, wanted the dedication service to be held in their church. He said they would be responsible for the program and supply the food for the occasion.

> This they did in grand style. Miguel and his wife Aurelia composed a hymn in Totonac using the hymn tune, "Holy Bible Word of God," for it. The quartet that sang the new hymn in Totonac did an excellent job. The service lasted for two hours. A small group of fellow translators went there with me. Mr. Lopez, the director of the Mexican Bible Society, came to officially present the new translation to the Totonac audience. The church was full to overflowing with believers from many of the surrounding villages. They had killed seventy chickens and two pigs. What a sight to see all of the women with their white clothes busily preparing the meal in large cauldrons out in the open. What was most impressive was the joy those believers from Zongozotla showed in all of this.

When Herman left Nanacatlan to assume the position of Government Man, he and Bessie experienced a deep sense of loss. They realized they would never again return to live in Nanacatlan with the friendly Totonacs they had grown to love, nor would they ever again live in that beloved, old stone house.

> In 1959 we finally left that house for the last time. It was a house where we spent ten of our most enjoy-able years among the Totonacs. As far as I knew, no one ever lived in that house again. Indalecio and the people in the town wanted us to return and they kept

it clean as they waited for us to come back. But after her heart stopped on the operating table, Bessie was in no shape to live in primitive conditions.

In the spring of 1959, I, with fellow colleague Dick Blight, had to deliver the devastating news to Herman that their son Johnny had died. In his memoirs Herman said:

> In 1959 while we all lived in Mexico City, catastrophe struck when our nine-year-old Johnny died. I was so overwhelmed with grief, I could not stop crying. "Lord! How could you let this happen?" It took a long while, but finally there came that peace that only God can give.[39] [See Chapter 1 for more details.]

Herman was to work in government relations from 1957 until 1964. During that time he took occasional trips out to the Totonac area, mostly during the summer. When he did return for a visit to Nanacatlan, he was pleased to discover that, in his absence, some of the young men who came to visit him had become good storytellers, and Herman began recording them.

> The best storyteller was Juan Castaneda. Unfortunately he was a sickly little fellow with a weak voice. He also could hardly see. Although he told his stories in a monotone, there was nothing weak about the dynamic content of his stories.[40] Once while I was recording one of his stories, my recorder malfunctioned. When I asked Juan to record the same story again, I was amazed that he repeated it verbatim the second time. This told me many of the stories we were

---

39 In remembering this tragic event, Dan Aschmann said that, after Johnny's death, his mother never regained her strength and emotional reserves to continue homeschooling as she had done in the past.

40 Recording and then printing the legends and stories of an ethnic group is a good way to help new readers have something interesting to read.

getting were stylized and memorized as part of their folklore to be passed on from person to person without much innovation.

Speaking of recorders, Herman's first was a bulky wire recorder he used to record Bessie singing the new Totonac hymns. In those early days, a spool of steel wire was magnetized in the same way that magnetic tape is used in more modern recorders. Herman was pleased to learn that many in the community were taking the gospel seriously and applying Christian principles to their daily lives, including their marriages.

Mariano Luna was the first believer in Nanacatlan. He was then an old man with teenage children. When he committed his life to Christ, his commitment was total. He told me that now he was a follower of Christ there were two things he wanted to do before he died. One was to be baptized and the other was he wanted to be legally married to his wife with whom he had been living for some twenty years.

One day, without saying anything to us, he took off with his spouse for Zapotitlán to be civilly married in the town hall. He also took his three children along so that they could be witnesses. Zapotitlán was the township to which Nanacatlan belonged and the place where people could be married civilly and their marriages registered. I have wondered what the town authorities thought of such a belated civil marriage.

During their time of service in Mexico City, Herman and Bessie were often surprised by visits from their many Totonac friends. Some had a favor to ask; others just came to visit. One day a Totonac lady from Coxquihui, who was also living and working in Mexico City called on them.

> This lady wanted most to tell us that she had bought one of the Highland Totonac New Testaments and started reading it. At first she didn't know what to make of it. However, gradually, as she kept on reading, she became convinced this was a personal message for her from God Himself. "Because," she said, "it smacked of the truth" and she wanted that salvation it talked about and to give her life to God in a new way.

Such stories of how the Totonac New Testament was making an impact on individual lives were becoming more frequent. Once when Manuel and Herman visited the village of San Pedro Camocuautla, they came across another old Totonac woman whose story was similar to the lady from Coxquihui. After reading and reading the New Testament, the old lady was convinced this was God's book. She told Herman and Manuel how her daughters had bought the New Testament and how they would read it to her. But the old lady didn't just want to listen to her children read to her. She sensed that they got something good out of reading it by themselves, so she wanted them to teach her how to read. They did. When she met Herman and Manuel she wanted them to know that the more she read the book the more she was convinced this book was from God.

On one occasion, Herman had a visit from a Totonac man from the village of Ixtepec. The man's name was Elijio, and he came to ask Herman if he would write a letter in Spanish for him. The man wanted the letter addressed to the resident priest in Zapotitlán. He wanted the priest to know that when he last visited Ixtepec, where he had gone to bless Elijio's house, it didn't work. Elijio explained to Herman that someone had cast a spell on him and his family. That is why he had paid the priest to bless it in order to take away the hex. Elijio said he knew his house was hexed from certain evidences, like the bones of a turkey he unearthed next to the wall of the house. Further, someone had stolen his cow, and Elijio believed that was part of the hex. Also, Elijio's sons were still having marital troubles, for which he wanted a remedy. There were other misfortunes as well.

Elijio asked Herman to write all the problems he was having in a letter, and to send it to the priest and ask him to please come again to his house and do a better job of exorcising it. He was willing to pay him whatever he asked.

> I was at a loss to know what to say. He did have a problem as he couldn't speak Spanish and the priest couldn't speak Totonac. I finally told him the priest would know who wrote the letter from my grammatical flaws that I, as a foreigner, would surely make in my Spanish writing.

> Then I asked whether he had ever prayed to God directly for help. No he hadn't. I asked if he would like me to show him how to do that. For Elijio this was something new. How could he pray to someone you can't see or feel or know is visibly like the statues of the saints? He said: "Sure." So, sentence by sentence I had Elijio repeat the little prayer I made up in Totonac. I forget what I actually said, but I brought in repentance and confessing his sins to God, as well as thanking Him for letting Jesus die on the cross so that he could be forgiven. I then had him ask God to please help him find a solution for his problems. Last of all I had him thank God for being merciful to him in listening to his prayer. It was as simple a prayer as I could make.

> We talked a bit more and then he said, "I don't want to forget that prayer. Please help me pray it again." So,

sentence by sentence, I tried to repeat the prayer just as I had said it before. Then I told him that a better way than memorizing that prayer was to just talk to God using his own words and believing that He really would be there listening. You can't see or feel God because He is a spirit, but He is real, He is always right there beside you.

Elijio left and I didn't see him again for five or more years. Then in 1960, Manuel Arenas and I were going from town to town to see if people were buying and reading the Highland Totonac New Testament that had just been printed. In Ixtepec we stayed a few days with a Christian family.

While we were there, a young man came and said his father wanted Manuel and me to come and eat at his house. To my surprise the father of the family was none other than Elijio! He told us that God had answered the prayer I had taught him years before. He had also started meeting with the few believers in that town. He had bought a Totonac New Testament and was reading it. Simple suggestions about spiritual matters often can produce great results.

The church in Zapotitlan.

13

Fishing for Words

A few months after Johnny's funeral, Herman and Bessie decided to spend another furlough year (1959-1960) in Sulphur Springs, Arkansas. Besides providing a space for healing, Sulphur Springs proved to be a profitable time for Bessie, who took two semesters of studies at John Brown University in Siloam Springs. Herman admitted it was time consuming for Bessie to commute sixty miles round-trip every day, but Bessie was determined to get her degree in anthropology.

Their children, Rick and Dan, also had the experience of becoming reacquainted with their American culture by attending a middle school. For high school, Rachel, Tim, and Rob drove by car each day to

Noel, Missouri (five miles from Sulphur Springs). And at both ends of that furlough year Herman and Bessie spent the two summers studying at SIL in Norman, Oklahoma. In the fall of 1961, Herman and Bessie returned to Mexico City taking only Dan and Rick with them. Rachel and Tim stayed behind to attend high school in Oklahoma City and to live at Wycliffe's children's home. Later Rob went to Tennessee Temple College in Chattanooga, and Tim would study to be a biomedical technician at Central State College in Oklahoma. The Aschmanns' return to Mexico City coincided with SIL's move from the cramped, overcrowded Kettle to new offices and expanded living apartments at their new center in Colonia Tlalpan.

> Not only were we pleased to have a new apartment all
> to ourselves, we had a bonus surprise to learn that for
> the first time SIL began a school on the new center
> for the children of our SIL members. This meant Rick
> and Dan could spend their school year living with us.
> And once again I kept busy with government relations
> affairs.

Herman's skill and winsome ability in government relations was well known. But so was Herman's skill as a linguist and Bible translator, which in reality was his first love. Thus, whenever there was an opportunity to visit the Totonac area, or to study the Totonac language, Herman took it. In the fall of 1962 he and colleague Kent Wistrand took a month-long survey of the Totonac speaking area surrounding the towns of Papantla and Coyutla. The dialectal information they collected convinced Herman the Papantla dialect was different enough for the necessity of translating a New Testament in Papantla Totonac, just as he had done in Highland Totonac.

Also, in 1962 Herman spent a week with Larry and Doris Puckett in Mecatlan, where there was a thriving Totonac church.[41]

---

41 Larry and Doris Puckett worked with the Unevangelized Fields Mission and became good

Joaquin, the pastor of the church, was a young man whom the Pucketts had sponsored to attend their mission Bible school. When Joaquin graduated, he returned to become the pastor of the Mecatlan congregation. A year later, in 1963, the Pucketts again invited Herman to Mecatlan, this time to give a series of talks on the Holy Spirit in Totonac. While he was there, Herman and Larry visited one of the Indian families. As they walked the uneven trail, Herman, who wasn't watching as they talked together, stepped into a mole hole. Herman said, "It was my left foot and when I heard it crack, I knew the ankle was definitely broken."

There was, of course, no one in Mecatlan to set the bone and immobilize it with a plaster cast. Larry, who had his light Piper Cub, said he would fly Herman to a doctor in Poza Rica. However, the airstrip was an hour's walk down from the village. The only way for Herman to get to the plane would be on mule back. After a painful, jerky, mule ride and then a flight to Poza Rica, they reached their destination.

> The doctor took an X-ray of my ankle bone and saw that it was broken in a V shaped crack but not out of place. After putting my whole lower leg in a cast, Larry immediately drove me to our Tlalpan headquarters in Mexico City. (His car was stored at the airfield.) And who should I find there but our colleague, Dr. Bob Crawford.

> That night the pain in my ankle became so unbearable I phoned Dr. Bob. He asked if I could feel my big toe. When I told him I couldn't, he said, "I think the cast is too tight. Cut the cast off!" When I did, I felt immediate relief.

As a result of Herman and Kent Wistrand's linguistic survey,

---

friends with Herman and strong supporters of the Totonac work in Mecatlan. They encouraged the reading of the translated Totonac New Testament in their literacy classes.

Herman and Bessie began to think of moving to Papantla, Veracruz, to live among the Lowland Totonacs. Herman wanted, once and for all, to determine if that dialect was truly different enough to need a New Testament translation of its own. In spite of Herman's leg still being in a (new) cast, he drove to Papantla to begin the first phase of learning the Papantla Totonac language. Dan and Rick were now attending the school in the Tlalpan headquarters and living in the children's home. While Herman and Bessie were in Papantla scouting out the area, they happened to meet Juan Gutierrez, a wealthy rancher from Papantla.

> I first got to know Juan on our survey when Kent and I happened to stop by his ranch. When we first met, he told me he had heard about our work with the Highland Totonac from a neighbor of ours who knew us when we were living in Zapotitlán.
>
> He liked what we were doing for the Totonacs and offered his help. I told him Bessie and I needed to find a Totonac village to live in. Could he help us do that? He immediately took us to the town hall in Papantla and introduced us to the authorities. He also requested they write a letter to the town fathers in a little Totonac village called Escolin recommending us and requesting that they please find a place for us in which to live and study.

When Herman and Bessie went to Escolin, the town fathers received them graciously and gave them a spare room in the schoolhouse for their living quarters. Herman then told Juan they now needed two good helpers who were fluent in both Spanish and Totonac to help them in their search for words to include in the dictionary. To Herman and Bessie's amazement, Juan sent two of the best bilinguals for that purpose. Herman and Bessie were now in business.

In addition to their translation work, Herman and Bessie had previously printed a dictionary for the Highland Totonac. This would be their base to systematically elicit equivalent Papantla Totonac words and sentences. They had long since jettisoned their bulky wire recorder for two little tape recorders that used small, three-and-a-half-inch spools of tape. Bessie used as her base all the words on the Spanish-Totonac side of the Highland Totonac dictionary, asking for their equivalents in Papantla Totonac. Herman then exhausted the Totonac-Spanish side to do the same. In a month they had filled 103 of those little spools of magnetic tape.

Herman said all they did was record the questions they asked in Spanish and the answers the language helpers gave them in Totonac. In that way Herman and Bessie systematically compiled a large assortment of words and sentences in a fairly short period. However, it would take Herman and Bessie two years of transcribing, sorting out, and cross-checking many of the words with their two language helpers. For example, when Herman got the words *akpakat* and *taknu* for "hat," he asked his language helpers where the word *taknu* was used. They said, "Only in towns like Huitlapan, Ixtepec, and other towns." Since the word for "hat" in Nanacatlan was *akpakat*, Herman had to make this distinction in the Lowland phrase book he was preparing.

> In the end we compiled over 3,000 entry words for
> our dictionary. To put the words in alphabetical order
> I filled nine shoe boxes of 3 by 5 slips, one for each
> word. In those days there were no computers to help
> us. We also had slips that described the conjugation
> of verbs and other interesting grammatical features.
> Their numerical system had to be highlighted as it
> was unique.[42] So was the way Totonacs looked at

---

42 The system for counting depends on the shape of the object. There is a "general" prefix for counting. But there is also a prefix for something long and thin, a different one for round objects (ball, hour, orange, etc.), one for humans, and another for animals. There are over twenty prefixes listed for numbers in Herman's Totonac dictionary. If a lady in the market has both oranges and

colors, body parts, and spatial notions. When I had sorted out all the words we wanted as dictionary entries, I composed the master copies of each page of the dictionary on my big IBM Selectric typewriter. A friend had given us the money to buy that electric typewriter just for that purpose. Now all this can be done on a computer. What a difference composing pages on a computer can make in time and effort.

When Herman and Bessie first went to Escolin, there were no sidewalks in the village, and most of the time the ground was soggy and muddy. When Herman walked around in that dampness, the new cast on his leg began to fall apart. One afternoon Juan Gutierrez arrived to give Herman a message. The SIL office in Mexico City had phoned Juan to ask if he could get a message to Herman that his mother had died.

When Juan told us the news I knew I had to get to my mother's funeral as quickly as possible and drove immediately to Mexico City. When I arrived, I felt it would look improper for me to board the plane with a tattered and muddied leg cast. So before going to the airport to catch my flight, I cut it off. After arriving in New York and telling my sister Mildred what I had foolishly done, she was sure I had done damage to my leg and it would not fully heal without a cast. However, I felt I had to take the risk since I couldn't be bothered with another cast. I really should not have done it, but God took pity on me. I made it back to Mexico and Bessie in good shape, and we were soon at it again in Escolin fishing for words.

---

bananas for sale, a Totonac speaker can simply say "two" with the proper prefix and she will give the customer bananas every time.

During the summer of 1966 Herman again had to work as SIL's government relations man. But after several months, the director in Mexico City felt Herman and Bessie needed a rest. He suggested they take a furlough in Oklahoma City to be with their older children. Herman agreed, but it would be a working furlough. Herman had long wanted to do a revision of the Highland New Testament with Manuel, but Manuel was doing other things; namely, establishing his Totonac Bible School and Cultural Center.

> This time we took Felipe Ramos with us to see if I could, while there, finally get to revise the New Testament with him. We also wanted Felipe to start translating a Bible story book of the Old Testament personalities that are mentioned in the New Testament. However, we weren't there long before Manuel Arenas phoned from Mexico saying that he desperately needed Felipe to return immediately to Mexico to help him. Someone had donated the money for him to buy the land on which to build his Bible school for his fellow Totonacs. He wanted Felipe to get Pedro Garcia and his wife Josefa in Nanacatlan to come and help him. He also wanted Felipe to see if he could get Alberto Cano from Zongozotla to do the same. There was the jungle to clear and the coffee trees to plant as the school's cash crop. He also wanted Felipe and Alberto to find students for his school and to be his first teachers. What else could Felipe do but return to Mexico.

Herman said he hated to lose Felipe, but in reflection said that without Felipe their time in Oklahoma City was a time of rest for him. But not so for Bessie. For her it was a busy time as she took classes in anthropology at Oklahoma University. When Herman and Bessie did return to Mexico City, the director asked Herman if he could, once again, take care of some urgent government matters. Finally, that fall they were again in Escolin finishing their search for words.

In 1983 Herman sent me a letter in which he outlined some of the early problems he and Manuel faced as they ventured into unknown translation territory. The letter is refreshing for his candor and willingness to admit he had a lot to learn about producing an idiomatic translation. Herman wrote that when Manuel began helping him to learn his distinct Highland variant of the Totonac language, they soon tried their hand at translating some New Testament verses into Totonac.

> Manuel knew a little Spanish, and I knew a little about how to translate meaningfully and dynamically into another language. In those early days all we had of source material were the English King James and the Spanish Devalera versions of the Bible. No one had yet produced any translation helps and text books on translation techniques. I was just beginning to analyze the ins and outs of Totonac grammar and syntax. I have to admit that I did a poor job with those first attempts. Yet one learns to translate by doing it just as any writer learns by writing. Also I had a dedicated helper who wanted to learn.

> Totonac phonemics is relatively easy, and I mastered that quickly, except for some of the subtleties of Totonac *sandhi*. Since sandhi has also to do with grammar, style and meaning, as a foreigner I'll never fully master that. Let me give you an inkling of what this sandhi is. It might be compared to the final /r/ some Bostonians add to English when they find a vowel at the end of a word. I'm sure you've quickly identified such New Englanders when they do that.

In English this has no meaning. It's purely a [dialec-
tal] quirk. But there are some junctures within and
between words in English that certainly do. Compare
the words: "night-rate" and "nitrate." The syllable
division or juncture between the /t/ and the /r/ makes
the difference. When spoken, it is only that difference
that changes the meaning of these two English words.

Herman admitted all this was rather complicated, but concluded
his letter with a reminder that translating the scriptures for the
Totonacs depended on his being able to comprehend and manage the
language's complex grammatical system.

After working with Manuel, Florencio, Agustin,
Felipe and others it is a privilege to find such ethnic
people who still have a deep appreciation for their
mother tongue even after they have learned Spanish
well. After working with these very bright people
I now knew just where my role as a Bible translator
lay. It is to encourage those who could respond to the
challenge of translating God's Word in their mother
tongue and make them feel as if they could do it.

This, however, means the challenger must also master
that tongue well enough to say, "Good job," when the
national translator does well and to be able to also show
him [or her] where he can or could do better if he hasn't
done so well. I remember how Florencio, thinking he
had done well, would wilt when I couldn't appreciate
something he had done. At the same time, he knew I
was the only one who could keep him from making
mistakes in the translation as well as the only one
capable of knowing when to encourage him. He needed
and wanted that. Such is the role of a Bible translator.

Herman shares his linguistic and cultural acumen in a writer's seminar.

14

Born with Ink in His Veins

Historians writing about the spirit of the sixties and early seventies point to one year, 1968, when the antiestablishment uprisings from January to December were most turbulent. Yet juxtaposed between these clashes, the sixties and seventies produced some of world's most important technological breakthroughs.

Dr. Christian Barnard performed the first heart transplant. Pocket-size hand calculators were all the rage, and TV-size microcomputers were replacing Selectric typewriters. And there was a quiet bestseller hitting the market called *The New English Bible*. This was produced by a group of British scholars who translated the entire Bible directly from the ancient texts into modern English for the first time. However, since it did not have the resonant phrasing of the King James Version, the new volume wasn't without its critics.

While Herman's memoirs are a testimony to his pioneer spirit of quietly offering a new way of life for the Totonacs through the translated scriptures, there is no mention of his feelings about the new way of life the youth of his own culture demanded. Instead, his focus was the Totonacs. In 1967 he had high hopes of spending the summer in Nanacatlan. However, due to medical problems, this was not to be. During the years 1967 through 1969 Herman again worked in government relations. Their son Rick attended the school at the SIL center. But since the school only went through ninth grade, Dan lived in the children's home in Oklahoma City in order to attend Putnam City High School. Early in 1970, Manuel Arenas invited Herman and Bessie to come and live in a house next to his Bible school in La Union. This was his gift to them for as long as they wanted to live in it. Herman noted it was an ideal place for him to finish putting together his Papantla

Totonac dictionary that was almost ready for printing.

> What a day that was when I handed it in to be printed.
> It didn't take many years before that edition was sold
> out. When I told my friend Juan Gutierrez that it
> would be dedicated to him, he gave me 500 pesos to
> defray some of the printing costs.

In the summer of 1970, Herman and the family returned to
Norman, Oklahoma, in order for Bessie to finish her studies for a
bachelor's in anthropology at Oklahoma University. She received
that prized possession in June 1971. Their daughter Rachel was also
a student at Oklahoma University during that year. In 1971 Dan also
began his studies there. And when Herman and Bessie returned to
Mexico, Rick lived in Norman for a year with a Mr. Davenport. When
it came time for Herman and Bessie to actually leave for Mexico,
some friends at their Baptist church in Norman replaced their old
car with a sturdy pickup truck with a camper shell on it.

> That pickup served us well for many years especially
> in my travels around the Papantla area. I took it
> everywhere, both where there was a road and where
> there wasn't one. Once, when I was in a remote area,
> the rear wheel, still attached to the axle, came off and
> rolled down the highway. It was a lonely road, but
> thankfully someone came along in his car and took
> me to Poza Rica. There I found a mechanic who went
> with me to where I had left the pickup. He took one
> look, picked up the wheel and axle and took it back to
> his shop. In a few days I had my pickup repaired good
> as new.

> Another time while traveling on a muddy dirt road
> I became mired down in a deep mud puddle. The

more the wheels spun around the deeper went the camper. As I sat there wondering what to do next, a truck with some oil well explorers came by and were only too happy to pull me out. Another time, as we topped a hill traveling on the highway going east towards Tulancingo, that same faulty back wheel and axle began making a scraping sound and I was afraid it might come off again. Although I was out in the country, I suddenly came across an auto repair shop. Those Mexicans are used to fixing old cars, and soon we were on our way again. The worst scare we had with that old camper was while we were driving on the highway from Apizaco to Mexico City. As we came down the steep incline that falls down into the valley of Mexico, half way down the brakes gave out. Thank God there were no cars in front of us. We had to crawl into Mexico City at a snail's pace using only the hand brake to stop or slow down.

In 1971, after Herman and Bessie had finished working on the Papantla Totonac dictionary, they wondered what they should do next. They had tried to find someone who would be interested in helping them translate the New Testament into Papantla Totonac, but found no one. Then, that year SIL was planning to have a Native Writer's Workshop at their Ixmiquilpan translation center. Herman was asked if there might be some talented Totonacs open to developing their abilities in the art of writing interesting stories in their mother tongue. There would be classes and experts to help them write their native stories and legends in the most appealing way possible.

Herman wrote to Herman Garcia, a Highland Totonac speaker from Zongozotla, asking if he would like to take the course. He wrote back saying he would be glad to come. Herman also asked his good rancher friend, Juan Gutierrez, if he could help him find a native

Totonac speaker from the Papantla area who would like go to such a workshop. Herman explained that anyone willing to go would have all his expenses paid but would receive no pay. This person would have to be someone who liked to tell stories and should know how to write them in an appealing way so others would want to read them.

Juan asked Herman to write a memorandum describing what was needed, and he would make copies for the schoolteachers and others. Unknown to Herman, Juan took his memorandum and published it in the Papantla newspaper. The next time Herman visited Juan, he told Herman what he had done. To Herman's utter surprise, there were fifteen aspiring writers wanting to go to the workshop!

Herman now faced the problem of knowing which one to choose. Fortunately the reporter from the newspaper helped him. He suggested Florencio Jimenez Juarez as the most talented. He was a Totonac who had written prizewinning poetry in Spanish and spoke both Spanish and Totonac fluently. Juan immediately sent someone to find Florencio so Herman could meet him.

> Florencio was quite a dapper little fellow. Except for
> his dark skin he didn't look or dress like a Totonac.

Florencio assured Herman he was enthusiastic about going to the workshop, but said he couldn't leave right then. Herman then gave him instructions on how to get to the SIL headquarters in Tlalpan. However, when the time came for Herman to leave for the Ixmiquilpan translation center, Florencio had not yet arrived. Believing he might yet come, Herman left instructions at the information desk for someone there to tell Florencio how to get to Ixmiquilpan by bus. They were also to tell him that when he got there he should phone Herman at the center in order for Herman to pick him up at the bus station.

Florencio arrived the day after Herman arrived, and after getting settled, Herman told him about the kind of stories he wanted him to write. Herman then introduced him to the other budding ethnic writers with whom he would be rooming, and left him with them. The next morning Florencio astonished Herman by handing him five pages of handwritten material in Totonac. Herman noted that his orthography in writing Totonac was a bit confusing, which made it difficult to read. Herman then asked Florencio to read it back to him as he recorded it on cassette tape.

> I had no trouble transcribing his text on my typewriter. When I did I was able to show Florencio the right letters he should use to write in Totonac.

Florencio's first narrative was how he had left his hometown for places unknown. He told about how he felt leaving his mother and family for the first time. He described his feelings about the bus ride to Mexico City. He wrote about almost getting lost trying to get to Tlalpan and about his relief in finally reaching Herman in Ixmiquilpan. Here was a Totonac opening himself up to write about his feelings in a way most Totonacs would never do. Herman was delighted because he saw in Florencio an ability to communicate in an interesting and personal way.

> I saw we had a genius on our hands. Surely he had been born with ink in his veins! When Florencio turned in his first manuscript, he mentioned how God and the seven guiding spirits had helped him find his way to Ixmiquilpan. [The seven guiding spirits are part of the Totonac belief system.] He also included some Catholic beliefs.

When Herman talked to him about the Catholic part, he told Florencio that even though most of the people at the workshop were Protestant followers of Christ, no one had any intentions of making him a Protestant.

If he was a true Christian, all we wanted was to help him become a better one. If he wasn't sure what it meant to be a true Christian, I told him I had a book I wanted to give him that could help him become one. I then gave him a copy of the Version Popular of the New Testament in Spanish. The outcome of that conversation was that a week later Florencio handed me an acrostic poem in Spanish. On the left of the page was my name: PEDRO ASCHMANN written vertically. After each letter was a line of prose in Spanish that expressed his appreciation for our having directed his footsteps to Christ so that he could trust in him alone as his Savior. There were other influences, I'm sure, that led him to make such a momentous decision. During that week some of the other Indian fellows must have talked to him about their faith in Christ. They had also taken him to hear pastor Venancio preach in the evangelical Otomi Indian church in Ixmiquilpan.

When the three-month course was over, Florencio had written over forty stories in Totonac. There wasn't much advice Herman could give him on how to improve them.

His stories were all handwritten which meant, in order to analyze them, I had to transcribe them. But it was a profitable exercise because typing off his handwritten manuscripts taught me a lot about the language. It also made me more and more aware that here was somebody I could trust completely in his consistently correct grammar and use of words. He wrote in an easy flowing way about his feelings, impressions, legends, customs and desires for his people. He even tried writing poetry in Totonac.

> As we worked with him, Bessie and I began to pray that
> God might give him the desire to be our co-translator
> of the New Testament into his mother tongue! Finally I
> asked him if he would like to do that with me. His answer
> was: "I've been waiting for you to ask me." I made it
> clear to him that the translation would be primarily his.
> I would only be his consultant and the one to help him
> in the hard to understand places as well as to check on
> accuracy and meaningfulness of the translation.

Before Florencio left for home, Herman loaded him up with four
versions of the Bible in Spanish and a Spanish edition of Lenski's commentary on the book of Mark. Herman challenged him to try to improve
on his techniques. Herman also told Florencio to spend his full time at
translation and challenged him to trust God for his finances.

> I told Florencio he would need some kind of financial
> support. I also told him that we just don't have enough
> of our own right now to help him, but would he be
> willing to trust the Lord to supply this need?

In Papantla, Florencio returned to his old job as a baker's helper
at night. During the day he attended the Papantla City high school.
In between times he translated. Not long afterward, a friend in
California wrote Herman to say he had been given a raise of fifty
dollars a month. Amazingly he said he and his wife didn't need that
money and asked Herman if he know of some need in the work where
this would be useful? Herman immediately wrote and told them
about Florencio who needed financial support so he could spend his
full time translating the New Testament into his mother tongue.

> Every month for the next four years, that couple sent
> fifty dollars to Florencio. What an encouragement
> that was to Florencio. To him that was a lot of money.

Herman and Florencio Jimenez just months before Florencio's tragic death.

Shortly after Herman received the letter from his friends in California, Dr. Baez Camargo, a Christian educator in Mexico City, asked Howard Klassen, then the associate director of SIL in Mexico, if he knew of some worthy, young ethnic co-translator who needed support. His Bible class wanted to support an ethnic Bible translator. Howard told him about Florencio. From then on, his Bible class sent him the equivalent of a hundred dollars a month. They insisted on meeting him, so one Sunday Herman took Florencio to Dr. Camargo's Sunday morning Bible class in Mexico City. Herman reported that Florencio made a great impression on those who were there with his intelligence and dedication. What was yet to be revealed to Herman was how Florencio's insight would revolutionize his understanding of the translation process, and how Florencio would become his teacher.

15

Give Me Your Soul

The challenge Herman gave Florencio was to make the translation of the Gospel of Mark into Papantla Totonac "his own." He wanted Florencio to grapple with the text and then write the translated text using the style and everyday language he would use as he spoke to his fellow Totonacs.

> Later when I reflected on how Manuel and I trans-lated the Highland Totonac New Testament, I realized I had conditioned Manuel (always the diplomat) into giving me answers he thought I wanted. As we worked across the desk from one another, I did the writing and Manuel, knowing what I wanted, gave me what I wanted.

> I later came to understand it should have been the other way around. Manuel should have written a first draft. What I was to learn is that if a person is forced to explain complex issues or concepts on the spur of the moment, the result of such an unreflective response is usually a poor translation. I did not want this to happen with Florencio. I challenged him, therefore, to give me a manuscript that came out of his own thinking and reflection. I wanted him to dig out the meaning of the words, to do research. I wanted him to give me his soul.

Herman was under no illusion about the difficulty of the nature of translation that lay ahead for Florencio. He knew the translator has two responsibilities. One is accuracy in discovering what the words of scripture really mean. The other is the art of expressing those meanings so the divine majesty and human verve of the Bible come through to the average person. Herman was also in Martin Luther's camp when Luther said, "To translate properly is to turn the spirit of a foreign language into the idiom [vernacular]. To express the idea in German [Totonac], one must ask the mother in the home, the children in the street, and the common man in the market place. Then people will recognize that someone is speaking to them in German [Totonac]." This is what Herman meant when he asked Florencio to give him his soul in the translation.

In just over a month, and much to Herman's surprise, Florencio handed him his handwritten, translated draft of Mark's Gospel. As Herman typed the translation into manuscript form, he saw that where the text dealt with straight narrative, Florencio had done wonderfully well. However, there were places where Florencio seemed to be in a hurry.

> In other places he didn't quite know how to handle foreign cultural items and certain strange words. His greatest problem however was his lack of background in the use of certain theological Bible words or ideas that were new or too complicated for him to fully understand. Then when he wanted to make something more understandable, he would interpret the passage incorrectly or he'd oversimplify.

> After a bit of orientation on how he could improve, I asked him if he would like to try doing a new draft of Mark. I told him he must give himself more time to do research and to try harder to understand what the Spanish Bible he was translating from was really trying to say. He must compare the different Spanish versions and read all that Lenski's commentary had to

say about the passages that sounded strange to him.

After that further explanation, Florencio returned to the translation desk determined to show Herman what a Totonac translator could do. Florencio not only made a new draft of the Gospel of Mark but he read it through several times to thoroughly edit it. Each time he made improvements. Even in Bible translation one can gain experience by just keeping on doing it. Florencio was a shining example of this.

When Herman and Bessie moved into the little house Manuel Arenas had given them next to his Bible school, it had been Herman's intention to be of some help to Manuel. However, Herman's time and energy were so occupied with compiling the Papantla Totonac dictionary and helping Florencio that there wasn't much time left to help Manuel, and in 1972 they moved.

We also needed to live closer to the Papantla area where I was doing a lot of traveling distributing the printed Gospels and making friends. That is why we decided to move to Xicotepec de Juarez. This was a large Spanish-speaking town on the highway between Mexico City and Papantla. We rented a house there from a kind German family, the Josephis. Xicotepec is 5,500 feet above sea level and a delightfully cool place to live. The Josephis were also the most congenial and gracious landlords. Our house was a hundred or more feet from theirs in a large compound covered with Norfolk pine trees. Another benefit of living in this cooler climate was an improvement in Bessie's health.

It was somewhere around that time that our son

Dan came to Mexico to visit us with four of his class-
mates. It was like going on a picnic for me to take
them to Manuel's Bible school and to Papantla to visit
Florencio. I took a photo of the boys standing around
the well in Florencio's backyard. He had whitewashed
the wall around the well opening and in Spanish wrote
the verse in John 4:13 where Jesus said: "Everyone
who drinks of this water will eventually be thirsty
again, but whoever drinks of the water I can give him
will never thirst again. Indeed the water I can give
him will become in him like a spring of water that will
keep on flowing on into life eternal."

On one of Herman's weekly visits to see Florencio, he told Herman
about his attempts to witness to his aged grandmother about putting her complete trust in Christ as her Savior. But the grandmother
would tell Florencio she was just too old to change or understand
what he was talking about. Florencio asked Herman how he could
best convince his old grandma of the importance of calling on God
to forgive her and save her for heaven. Herman simply said, "If words
don't seem to reach into her inner being, maybe you should just show
her how much you love her." Herman reminded Florencio his life had
been changed, and if he could demonstrate that, she might see the
hand of God in his life and feel the need for such a change in her own
life. Herman knew how much Florencio's changed life was affecting
his mother and siblings, and he hoped it might also have an effect on
his grandmother.

Several weeks after Florencio began reading and studying Lenski's
commentary on Mark's Gospel he was beginning to grapple with
some of the theological differences between Protestant and Catholic
doctrine. Lenski was a Lutheran, and in his commentary he discusses
transubstantiation. Catholic theologians believe that during Mass
the bread and wine of the Eucharist are transformed by consecration

into the actual blood and flesh of Christ. Reformed Protestants, on the other hand, believe no such miracle takes place and the elements only represent, in a symbolic way, Christ's flesh and blood.

So troubled was Florencio over this doctrinal divide that he went to Padre Manolo Jimenez, his local priest, and told him he no longer could partake of the Eucharist in the traditional Catholic way. To his surprise the good padre said, "Florencio, I know where your faith lies. Keep up the good work. I don't care whether you take the host at Mass or not." Padre Manolo told Florencio he should keep on attending Mass as an observer and should keep on translating the New Testament into Totonac. The padre said he felt many Catholic Totonacs needed to be able to read and understand what God wants to tell them in their mother tongue.

Padre Manolo was the director in Papantla of a pre-seminary for young men who wanted to become priests. They were given two years of study as a time of decision making for them to be absolutely sure the priesthood was for them. One day Padre Manolo invited Herman to come and talk to the young men about what it meant to be a Bible translator. He also wanted Herman to tell them what it meant to be truly converted to Jesus Christ.

> He told me to feel free to come to his school if I ever needed a place to stay overnight. One morning, after staying overnight at his school, he told me he held Mass every morning for the students, some neighbors and a few nuns, and would I like to worship with them that morning. I said yes. As I sat in the back row he gave a little message and then wiped the goblet in preparation for Mass. Then to my surprise he said: "Would the professor care to come and partake with us of the Eucharist?" I knew he was sincere so I went forward. He quoted the passage where it says: "This is my blood shed for you." Then to my amazement he

handed me the goblet containing the wine and told me to drink some of it. Then he did the same for the host as he gave it to me to eat. Only after I returned to my seat did the rest of the congregation come forward and partake of the elements in the traditional Catholic way. I wondered what the people thought when he invited me to come forward and partake of the elements. After the service I asked him why he had done it. He gave me a hug and said: "You are my brother in Christ and I wanted you to know that."

When the Gospel of Mark was ready for printing, Herman happened to talk with Dr. William Wonderly, a consultant with the United Bible Society (the publisher), who asked about Florencio's progress. Dr. Wonderly had taken a liking to Florencio and, like Herman, saw his potential. Dr. Wonderly suggested that Herman take a copy of the finished Gospel of Mark to the Catholic bishop of the diocese of Papantla. He told Herman to ask the bishop if he would like to have a competent Catholic Totonac speaker read it; and if he found anything they thought should be changed, the Bible Society would gladly change it.

Herman thought this was a good idea and first went to visit Padre José Gonzalez, the senior resident priest in Papantla, to get his help. Herman told him why he wanted to see the bishop and asked how he should best go about making an appointment to see him. As soon as Herman introduced himself to Padre José, the padre said, "You are just the person I have wanted to meet." Some months before, the padre had attended a small linguistics course that SIL gave at the Tlalpan center. While he was there, he learned what SIL's goals were and liked what he heard and saw of the Bible translators he met. During the course of conversation, someone mentioned that Herman and Bessie Aschmann were working on a translation of the New Testament into the Papantla Totonac language. When he learned that, Padre José told Herman he had very much wanted to get to know him and to offer his help in any way he could. Padre José's response to Herman after he had finished reading the translation of the Gospel of Mark was, "I do not need to take it to the bishop for his approval. I trusted you and know that whatever you translated of the Bible, I and my fellow priests will encourage the Totonacs to buy and read it."

> The Bible Society printed a thousand copies of Florencio's Gospel of Mark. To our amazement they were all sold in four months. Most were sold by the priests. Padre José had a stack of them on the table they kept at the front door of the church where they sold their own Catholic literature and other items. To keep the priests who lived in the area supplied with Gospels of Mark, I went to visit them in my camper. That way I also got to know some of the teachers in the rural schools on my many journeys.

Like any author, reader interest in one's work gives encouragement and validation to one's effort. And such was the case for Florencio. The sales of the Gospel of Mark greatly encouraged him. It also showed that what he was doing was of value to many Totonacs, who weren't aware of the whole gospel story.

At that time, Felipe Ramos had a weekly fifteen-minute radio program in Highland Totonac. It was aired out of a small radio station in Poza Rica. Herman wrote about it in an October 1976 letter to his financial partners and friends in the States.

> It is Sunday morning. I'm sitting listening to the radio with a few tears of joy. The reason for my happiness is because it's Padre Miguel's radio program and our Totonac friend Natalio is reading from the Papantla Totonac Gospel of Mark. It's about the rich, young

ruler: "Who then can be saved?" Just think of all those Totonac Indians listening! Then along comes Felipe Ramos' program in Highland Totonac on the same station. It is aired to reach the Highland Totonac audience in their dialect.

After the message, Felipe dubbed in Bessie and Manuel singing a duet in Totonac taken from one of the old Victrola records made way back in 1947. On many transistor radios up in those cloud-shrouded mountains simple folk were hearing them sing in Totonac about the grace of God, perhaps for the first time. It sounded so appealing!

It was once against the law in Mexico to broadcast religious programs on the radio in Spanish. For nine years Felipe Ramos got around that because his program was in Totonac, not Spanish. Then, because of finances and because it was too risky for the radio station to keep airing them, his programs were terminated. Over the years, Felipe continued to pray that God would give him another chance to broadcast in Totonac, that chance came in 2005.[43]

By 1976 Florencio had finished translating the four Gospels, Acts, and Romans. The United Bible Society printed a thousand copies of each book. By 1979, when the whole New Testament was printed, those six books had been all sold out and were in the hands of Totonac speakers. Herman said they were fortunate the Totonac language only requires an alphabet that is quite similar to that of Spanish, although some of the letters have slightly different sound values in Totonac than they do in Spanish. Most mother tongue speakers of Totonac, who have learned to read Spanish, don't have much difficulty reading

---

43 As of 2005 the radio program that was once called "The Totonac Cultural Hour" is now called "Good News for the Totonacs" (*Las Buenas Nuevas Para los Totonacs*). The Mexican government has changed the laws on religious broadcasting. Felipe has more liberty to present the gospel. The hour-long program includes Totonac ethnic music and readings in Totonac from the translated scriptures as well as community announcements.

their language with those same letters. Of course, if they are not mother tongue speakers of Totonac, they will certainly find it difficult to read that language correctly no matter what alphabet is used. Then on October 30, 1976, Herman wrote another letter to his ministry partners. This time the joy he had shared just days earlier was shattered. Herman's letter began, "FLORENCIO IS DEAD!"

*Herman and some young Totonac men take
a scenic break along a narrow mountain ridge.*

16

Please Never Come to Visit Me Again

Like God's servants in the Old and New Testaments and throughout the history of the Church, Herman and Bessie experienced moments of the dark night of the soul. After Johnny's death, the wound in Bessie's heart never fully healed. In their humanity, they grappled with the inevitable question of "Why?" However, over time and by God's grace, they affirmed God's faithfulness in their lives and with joy moved ahead with the work God had given them to do among the Totonacs. Part of Herman's joy was working with Florencio. He expressed this in his March 1973 newsletter when he was fifty-nine.

> The other day I said to Florencio, "At the rate we are going, God can help us finish in five years." Florencio nodded and said, "Why not make it four?" Florencio is an exceptionally talented young man. He has already translated over a third of the New Testament.

Herman would later write that, in four and a half years, Florencio became an excellent exegete[44] of the New Testament as well as a self-taught Bible translator. Florencio also remained close friends with Dr. Baez Camargo, whose Bible class supported him monthly, and with Dr. Bill Wonderly of the United Bible Society. A year later, in 1974, Herman wrote another newsletter to bring his prayer and financial supporters up to date. He began by inviting his readers to visit Bessie and him in their new home in Xicotepec de Juarez. Herman said it was an old house with a lovely patio and a guest room. But then, as an afterthought, he mentioned the house had a leaky roof and some

---

44 An exegete is a person who can explain or analyze a text.

termite dust.

> Bessie's heath is much improved now that we are living at this higher altitude (5,500 feet). Living here makes it easier for me to take the sixty-mile trip to Papantla to see Florencio and make my rounds selling the Gospels and dictionaries. I try to do this every other week. Our main thrust is to give the Lowland Totonacs their New Testament within the next three years.

> The book of Acts has been given a final okay for printing and Florencio has given me his first draft of the Epistle to the Romans. When he and I were talking over the difficulties in this book he said, "Paul has given me a clear grasp of the *faith* part of salvation. It can help others. Let's get this book printed right away."

If you weren't paying close attention to Herman's letter, you might have missed the longing he had in his heart for Nanacatlan.

> As I look out over our empty patio it gives me a feeling of loneliness. Seclusion is ideal for desk work, but we miss having the Totonacs around. When I go to the market I am always on the alert to catch someone talking Totonac or to see a familiar face. Many mountain Totonacs come to this market town, and we want to make ourselves and our lovely home available to them.

Then on October 30, 1976, Herman's life was once again shattered in ways that were beyond reason and that he could never have expected. His newsletter began with the heartbreak.

> FLORENCIO IS DEAD! This is a hard letter to write, but we wanted you to know right away. Our beloved

Florencio has been murdered by one of his clos-
est friends. Florencio had often talked to his school
friend Roberto[45] about turning his life over to Christ.
But Roberto was always resistant, to the point that he
once told Florencio if didn't stop talking to him about
changing his ways he would kill him. On October
29, Roberto was put in jail for a serious crime. The
next day Florencio went to see his friend and post
his bail. On the way through the woods together
to catch his bus home, Florencio must have made
Roberto angry as he again tried to persuade Roberto
to give his life to Christ. In a rage, Roberto picked
up rocks and savagely stoned Florencio to death.[46]
When we got the news my mind refused to think.
When I realized it was true, I was overwhelmed with
grief. I wasn't thinking of the New Testament not quite
finished, or the fun it was in working with a genius.
Nor was I thinking about that young enthusiastic life
so full of promise and joy as he grew in Christ, or that
all this was now senselessly snuffed out. No, I was just
completely overcome and shattered by my own sense
of acute personal loss. How could we lose someone
who could love us like Florencio! When we shared our
faith in Christ with him, it was never anything shal-
low. He could open up his innermost being to us, and
this freed us to do the same.

Never have we seen anyone drink so deeply and freely
of the saving grace of God as he did. The tenderness
with which he expressed his appreciation that Bessie

45 Not his real name.
46 Roberto was put in jail for killing Florencio, but his father paid to have him released. Roberto then left Papantla to live in Mexico City.

and I had been God's instruments in showing him the Way seemed like something God himself wanted us to know. That he understood and appreciated the freeing love of God showed up in the way he translated God's Word so that others would know about it as well. He was so much a part of us and now he is gone!

At the wake, neighbors came and went with food, others came to just sit and talk. Some came to chant prayers for the dead.

Florencio didn't need their prayers. He was already with Christ in that better place. Florencio died the way he might have wanted it, helping a friend come to Christ.

The morning Herman and Bessie drove to Papantla for the funeral, they reworked two of the Highland Totonac hymns into Papantla Totonac. It wasn't much; just a few stanzas. At the wake when Bessie sang "This World Is Not My Home" in Totonac, many of the sad faces ran with tears. Later one of the men asked them to come to the casket and sing more songs in Totonac. They sang "When the Roll Is Called Up Yonder," the only other song they knew in Lowland Totonac. When it was over, Herman wished they had more hymns in that dialect to sing for them. Finally, as Herman and Bessie dealt with the finality of Florencio's death, Herman questioned.

Where do we go from here? Who will help us finish the remaining work on the translation of the New Testament Florencio has left undone? The day he died he had his neatly-typed draft of the Epistle of 2 Peter on his desk. There were only five small books and the larger book of Revelation left for him to translate. Further, Florencio had intended to go through it again to do a final check and to rework some of the rough spots.

On the day of the funeral, four of Florencio's friends volunteered to try to help Herman finish what Florencio had left undone. Later they all dropped out but one. His name was Natalio. When he tried his hand at translating Peter's second epistle, Herman could see he did not have the gift of being an accurate and interesting writer in Totonac. However, Florencio's younger brother José said he had watched how Florencio translated and said he wanted to try his hand at it. Herman told him he was only fourteen years old and wasn't mature enough. But the next time Herman visited the family, José handed Herman his version of 2 Peter. Herman gave a copy to Natalio for his evaluation. Natalio said he made a few corrections that didn't amount to much and that it was well done.

At that point Herman asked the two of them to become his translation team. José, with his gift as a writer would translate his version of the Spanish text, and Natalio would polish it up. They proved to be just the right combination. In October 1977, a year after Florencio died, the book of Revelation was finally checked and ready for printing. The other New Testament books were being entered onto a computer. There were also always printouts for Herman to proofread—not once but two or three times. It would be six months to a year before those Lowland Totonacs would see the first printed copies, but the job was done.

> We owed so much to José and Natalio who have freely spent of themselves this last year to finish up something I wasn't at first fully sure they were capable of doing well. But they were! I'm sure they looked to God to help them find good solutions when they came to those places that at first seemed so impossible to translate. We owe even more to Florencio. He didn't stay to finish the perfect translation he was after. He

had intended, after finishing his draft of the whole New Testament, to go over the whole thing and give it his finishing touches. Natalio and Jose tried hard to follow in his footsteps, but Florencio had a way with Totonac words that none could approach. But the example he left behind had gripped those two and they did the best they could. After it was printed, it made for good reading. Three editions were printed totaling 3,000 copies in all. All those have now long ago been sold and are in the hands of Totonac readers.

When the Gospel of Mark was first printed in Papantla Totonac, (where there are over 80,000 Totonacs) Padre José Gonzales began recommending it to the other priests in the area. In four months the first thousand copies were sold out. Herman then had another thousand printed. Later, Matthew, John, Acts, and Romans were also one-thousand-copy editions.

Padre Jose de la Luz Silva, the resident priest in Coyutla, had known Florencio before he died and was impressed with the good work of translating he was doing. When he saw the Gospel of Mark in Papantla Totonac, Padre Silva contacted Herman to ask if he wouldn't please start working on a New Testament translation in Coyutla Totonac like the one he was translating for Papantla Totonac. Coyutla is a market town a hundred miles or so from Papantla that sits next to the Necaxa River. It is also where the mountains start to climb precipitously toward the west. It is home to some 48,000 Totonacs speaking another distinct variant in the Totonac family of languages.

At the time, Herman had to tell Padre Silva he was too busy working with the Papantla translation to think of getting involved in translating yet another New Testament. A few years later Padre Silva went to the Mexican Bible Society in Mexico City to ask if they would consider it. They, of course, referred him back to Herman. Then in 1977, Dr. William Wonderly of the United Bible Society, also with an office in Mexico City, phoned Herman to say that Padre Silva had talked to him about the need for a Coyutla translation of the New Testament. Dr. Wonderly gave his suggestions:

> Let's try to help this man. If you can get the right Totonac co-translators, the United Bible Society will take it on as one of their projects with you as facilitator and consultant.

Herman agreed and went to Coyutla to tell Padre Silva the good news. Herman arranged a date when Dr. Wonderly would also come to evaluate the situation. Padre Silva said he would have some of his bright young men who were bilingual in Totonac and Spanish to be considered as possible co-translators. Dr. Wonderly brought Dr. Bob Bascom,[47] a new consultant with the United Bible Society; and Dr. Bruce Hollenbach, translation coordinator from SIL, would be an observer. When the men arrived in Coyutla, Herman was surprised to meet over twenty Totonac young men, all eager to see if they could help in the translation effort. Bill Wonderly gave them orientation on translation techniques, and Herman taught them the alphabet they should all use to be consistent in their writing of Totonac.

Herman chose eight of them to translate different episodes in the Gospel of Luke. This was then printed in a booklet for others to read. Of the eight who translated parts of narratives on the life of Jesus, Agustin Juarez Duran showed exceptional talent. He was asked if he would be willing to dedicate all of his time to translate the New Testament with Herman as his consultant. He said he was willing. He was a farmer, and from then on, he hired others to till his fields while he put all his efforts into translating.

When Herman chose Agustin to be on the translation team, Padre

---

47 Bob Bascom was the son of Dr. Bert and Marvel Bascom, longtime Wycliffe translators who produced a translation for the Northern Tepehuan people.

Silva said he wanted to pay his wages for him to work full-time on translation. A few weeks later, Padre Silva was invited to hold Mass in a Catholic church in Laredo, Texas. As part of his homily he mentioned the new translation project among the Coyutla Totonac people. Afterwards someone stood at the door and collected two hundred dollars for the project. That took care of Agustin's wages for the first year. Later the United Bible Society contributed toward his support; and Dr. Baez Camargo's Bible class, which had been paying Florencio's wages in Papantla, also decided to support Agustin.

To get Agustin started, Herman gave him a copy of the Highland Totonac New Testament and three Spanish versions of the Bible to help him with insights on how to better understand some of the more difficult passages. Although Highland Totonac is quite different in many ways from the Coyutla Totonac dialect, Agustin occasionally found it helpful to refer to it for help in rewording or paraphrasing some of the more awkward passages.

> Agustin quickly learned to type, and it wasn't long before he had translated the Gospels. He was working like someone who had found something to live for and loved doing. He was clearly a born again evangelical, and wanted to especially make the verses that dealt with salvation unmistakably clear. And to our surprise we learned Agustin's wife, Micaela, also had a part in the translation.
>
> Agustin made a verse by verse back translation of his Totonac version into Spanish. In this way Bill could ask him questions or stop to discuss some passage with him. For example, when he came to the place where Jesus turned the water into wine, Bill congratulated him at a place where he had solved a knotty problem. Agustin had to admit it was Micaela who

had translated that chapter. Wow! What did we have here but a husband and wife translation team!

But just before the translation was to be completed, the goodwill and happy working relationship Herman had with Padre Silva and Agustin suddenly and unexpectedly collapsed. In 1982, without any explanation, Herman received a letter from Padre Silva that said, "I have asked Augustin to stop translating. Please never come to visit me again."

Herman and Bessie Aschmann, Tetelcingo, 1942.

17

Thinking More of God's Past Blessings

At sixty-four, Herman was still slim and looked as fit as he did at twenty. Bessie, on the other hand, was not as energetic at sixty-four as she once was. In Herman's words, "Her physical body was giving up on her which is causing her some depression." In 1980 Herman and Bessie came to the States for another furlough. This time it was to face the reality of Bessie's health.

> I could see Bessie seemed depressed at times although she tried to hide it. I believe much of this was physical. Her body just seemed to be giving up. Yet she still hoped to accomplish more for the Totonacs while she was still very much alive. Because of her deteriorating health, we stayed on in the States year after year until she finally came to realize we must consider retirement. To keep up with what Agustin was doing I would fly down to visit him every six months or so.

But then in 1982 Herman received Padre Silva's letter. At first reading, Herman simply stared at the letter in utter disbelief. It was a bombshell. For some time Herman was aware that many secular anthropologists were concerned about the influence SIL had in Mexico. Because he collaborated with Herman on the translation project, Padre Silva had unknowingly become involved in the controversy. So serious were the anthropologists that Padre Silva received a visit from one who told him to cut ties with Herman and SIL. Because of the pressure, Padre Silva felt his life's work was in jeopardy and told Agustin to stop translating. In the letter Padre Silva sent to Herman, he wanted Herman to understand he had nothing against him. In fact, he saw Herman as a good friend. It was that his job was at stake and he did not know what else to do.

After Herman received the letter, he immediately flew to Mexico City and called on a Mr. Tepox, an official with the United Bible Society. Herman asked Mr. Tepox to go with him to meet Padre Silva and try to persuade him to change his mind. Agustin didn't have much of the New Testament left to translate, but it was critical for the United Bible Society and Herman that Agustin finish the translation in order for it to be printed.

When Herman and Mr. Tepox reached Coyutla, Padre Silva, knowing why they had come, was courteous but said very little. He simply showed the men where they were to sleep and left saying he would talk to them later. At nine o'clock that night he returned. Padre Silva once again explained the pressure he was under from these various agencies. Herman and Mr. Tepox said they understood his problem but pleaded with the padre to let Agustin finish. Herman reminded Padre Silva that it would not be the Instituto Linguistico de Verano (ILV, Spanish for SIL) who would be the publishers but the Sociedad Biblica de Mexico (Mexican Bible Society). Finally Padre Silva said to Herman, "You and Agustin can finish your translation, but you must please never come to visit me again."

In 1986, with the Mexican Bible Society as its publisher, the green-covered Coyutla Totonac New Testament was finally printed. Herman thanked God for this. Later that year Herman flew again to Mexico. This time he went to Coyutla with a Mr. Prince who represented the Mexican Bible Society, delivering 200 copies to Padre Silva. On the day Herman and Mr. Prince arrived in Coyutla, they discovered it was a fiesta day, and a crowd of Totonac fellows had gathered in the patio of the church for the occasion.

Padre Silva publicly received the books and, as a gesture of appreciation, gave Mr. Prince a gift of 16,000 pesos (roughly $420 in those days) for those first 200 copies. They decided on a date when more representatives of the Mexican Bible Society might come and together publicly dedicate the Coyutla Totonac New Testament in the Catholic Church. Herman was later informed there was much interest and that pictures were taken of that event. However, before Herman left Coyutla, Padre Silva took him aside and told him once again to please never, ever come back to visit him. Padre Silva said he appreciated all that Herman had done, but it sure had gotten him into very serious trouble.

> Later I tried writing Padre Silva, but he never answered my letters. Agustin was also there that day when we delivered the New Testaments. I shook his hand, gave him a hug and told him how much I had appreciated his excellent work on translation. I then said goodbye for the last time. Later I tried writing him, but he wouldn't answer my letters. I had lost two wonderful friends. Or had I? They would never have severed our friendship if they hadn't been forced to do so. I do believe I'll see those two in heaven where we will openly be friends again.

Friends and colleagues were important to Herman. Thus to lose two good friends at once was a loss more painful than he would admit to himself. Yet, as often happens when we need it most, God sends a person or we receive a letter that gives us that extra boost of affirmation and encouragement. Herman received one such letter from Dr. Paulette Levy, who once headed the linguistics department of the University of Mexico. Dr. Levy said she was using the Papantla Totonac Dictionary, which Herman and Bessie had produced, as a reference in some fieldwork she was doing. She said she spent weekends in a Totonac village near Papantla living with a Totonac family. In her letter, she thanked Herman for the dictionary, which she said had helped her greatly. Then in her closing paragraph she wrote that at the house where she stayed she noticed the man of the house reading his Totonac New Testament every morning. She congratulated Herman for the good work he had done in producing a book that gave hope and changed the lives of so many Totonac people.

In 1982 God brought another gifted Papantla Totonac translator into Herman and Bessie's lives. The Mexican Bible Society forwarded a letter to Herman they had received from Alejandro Mendez San Martin. He was a native of a town near Papantla and wrote saying that Totonac was his mother tongue and he had finished translating much of the New Testament from Spanish into Papantla Totonac. He now needed advice on how to proceed in finding someone to publish it. The Mexican Bible Society suggested he write to Herman.

It turned out that Alejandro had committed his life to Christ through his contact with an Assemblies of God Church in Poza Rica. They saw his potential and sent him to a Bible school in Matamoras in the state of Tamaulipas. Herman wrote Alejandro telling him there was no need for him to produce another translation and sent him a copy of the already translated Papantla Totonac New Testament.

Alejandro answered saying he still wanted to finish his own translation since the one Florencio translated was for him "too much of a paraphrase." Herman said Alejandro wanted to produce a literal version using as his base the De Valera Spanish version. Herman noted this version uses some of the same kind of antiquated words that the King James Version does in English. Alejandro also sent Herman his draft of three of the Gospels.

> It was evident that when he wanted to be, Alejandro was an excellent communicator in Totonac. However, at the expense of intelligibility, there were many places where his translation resorted to a word for word literal equivalence with the Spanish version. He needed to understand it is the intended meaning *behind* the Spanish or Greek words that were inspired and not the form of the words themselves that he must

translate. When we translate from one language to another and find that translating word for word does not come out meaningfully, we must use a paraphrase to pass on what God wants us to know. In many places even his Spanish De Valera version did that.

Alejandro's hang-up was that he put too much emphasis on the very words as being inspired and not enough on the inspired meaning those words represent. I suspect Alejandro must have wrongly thought that to resort to a paraphrase was somehow to deviate from or add to the inspired meaning of the text. My dictionary says, "To paraphrase is to say the same thing but in other words." If to paraphrase is what it takes to get at the real meaning, so be it.

When Herman finally met Alejandro, he suggested he give up his translation of the New Testament for the moment and translate a good Bible story book of the people in the Old Testament who are mentioned in the New. Alejandro liked the idea, and Herman gave him two excellent Bible story books in Spanish as source material.

When Alejandro used his own words, he produced an interesting and an easily understandable book. It was printed in 1988 and has been well received.

Later Herman took Alejandro to the States where together they translated the Psalms. Herman tried to wean Alejandro away from his insistence on literalness, but with no success. To him the inspired scriptures were only inspired in an exact word-for-word way. Herman said the book was printed in 1990, but it made for heavy reading, and he doubted if it helped many readers. However, Herman was more agreeable with his work on Proverbs, which he said "came out somewhat better."

In the early 1980s, profound political and social changes were in the air for the Mexico Branch. Herman's 1982 letter from Padre Silva saying he was being pressured on all sides to end his relationship with Herman and the translation project was just the tip of the iceberg. It seemed there was daily criticism and harassment from the press, calling for the expulsion of the ILV. And then to add insult to injury, the Mexico State Department changed its policy of granting renewals for ILV worker's visas.

Visa problems were, of course, not a problem for Herman and Bessie and other longtime Mexico Branch workers since they had permanent resident papers. However, because of the growing political unrest, the Mexico Branch directorate decided to return the leased Tlalpan property back to the Mexican government ahead of schedule. In an October 1983 newsletter, Herman informed his prayer and financial partners of the change.

> Two years ago, when many of our colleagues could no longer get their visas renewed to continue working in Mexico [and many of our people had to leave the country], Wycliffe Associates of Tucson came to our rescue. They helped us build and establish a center of office buildings, library, study facilities, temporary apartments and more near the city [Catalina, Arizona, USA]. We now have facilities where we can bring indigenous co-translators to continue translating and the way has opened up for us to move to this new center. Lord willing, we will move into a mobile home (as many others are doing). I will have access to the Center library, to more commentaries and more time to help other translators with their problems. There will also be consultants to help Bessie with her literacy and linguistic projects.

A year later, in September 1984, Herman wrote to tell his ministry partners the Lord had enabled them to buy a "pretty," single-wide mobile home from a fellow translator. All he had to do was pick up the payments on the unit. He then said they had returned to Mexico in January for a month to sort out and dispose of most of their worldly possessions that were in storage there.

> While Bessie was doing this, I took off for the moun-
> tains of Totonac land. However, at sixty-nine years
> of age, my legs are no longer as trail worthy as they
> once were.

Herman's letter was a trip down memory lane. He wrote about his visit to Manuel at his Bible school and with Felipe Ramos who had the Highland Totonac radio program. He reminded his friends that it was in that dialect of Totonac that he and Manuel translated the first Totonac New Testament. To his delight he reported that the three New Testament editions in the three dialects as well as other printed materials were sold out. His next stop was to the Papantla area to visit Natalio, his principal distributor of the New Testament that was printed for that dialect.

> It was on this trip that I took the last of the 2,000
> copies of the printed New Testaments. When I returned
> again in August, they were all sold except for fifty
> copies. Natalio told me these were all he had left and
> were "much sought after." Natalio told me he was
> holding onto these fifty copies and would sell them
> only to those special people he thought were the hun-
> griest and would appreciate them the most. Good
> thought, Natalio!

When Herman and Bessie's son Rick and his wife Heidi Marie could not get visas for working in Mexico, they changed their field assignment to work with SIL in Colombia among the Yukpa Indians. In 1987 Herman and Bessie decided to take a much-needed rest from their work among the Totonacs and visited Rick and Heidi in Bogotá, Colombia. Herman reported they had some very good times together. However, a week after their arrival, Herman began to feel sick, and they returned home to Catalina. Within days after his return, Herman began coughing up yellow mucus from his lungs. Herman, who had rarely been ill throughout his adult life, was diagnosed with pneumonia, or so the doctors thought. Over the next several weeks, Herman's illness was severe enough for him to be hospitalized twice without any noticeable improvement.

> The doctors just didn't know what was wrong with me. They gave me all kinds of tests, but all were negative. As a last resort my doctor tested me to see if I had a rare disease called Mycobacterium (MAI)[48] also known as Mycobacteriosis. That culture took two months to incubate before the results were conclusive. It turned out that's what I had.

In February 1990 Herman wrote me a short note telling me he was taking three "rather toxic medicines" for his lung infection, but he said they did not seem to be doing much for him. And then his next paragraph showed me just how ill he was and why I called him a prince among men.

> I cough a lot and feel very weary at times. I don't have much drive any more to work on the dictionary I was making for the Coyutla Totonac. I find it much easier to just sit and read. This is something I never seemed to have enough time for. So, I must be content to slow down and read and think more of God's past blessings.

---

48 This is the same genus as the organism which causes tuberculosis.

Somehow that seems to suit Bessie's style as well. We
are two oldsters finding a new niche to settle into but
are still just as curious to find out what little surprises
God has in store for us next.

After four years of battling infections Herman went to a Jewish hospital in Denver to see if they might have a cure for his illness. They did
not have a cure. He continued bringing up matter from his lungs.

Finally my doctor said there was a new antibiotic I
could take in case the bacteria had become resistant to
the Cipro [the drug he had been taking]. Sure enough,
after taking that for two weeks I was completely cured!

In August 1991 Herman and Bessie celebrated their fiftieth wedding
anniversary. It was even more special because their children—Rob,
Tim, Rachel, Dan, and Rick came to Catalina to honor their parents.

Our anniversary celebration was a truly gratify-
ing experience. It felt good to be loved. Some of our
grandchildren came. My niece Karen Butler who lives
in Florida also came. Fifty years of marriage had
been the greatest education ever for Bessie and me.
We are now thoroughly used to each other, and the
more we live with each other the more we like each
other. In fact, we could no longer get along without
each other. And yet how different we were in many
ways. As to our goals in life, however, we are of one
mind. We are indeed thankful for all the busy years
we spent together living with the Totonacs and raising
our children.

Throughout Herman's correspondence there were frequent references to how proud he was of his children and, by 1994, of his
grandchildren. In a two-page, single-spaced letter to me dated July

1994, I read first about his daughter Rachel's son, Mike Redding, his first grandchild to graduate from college. And after a summer of work, he would be on his way to Stanford to begin his doctoral program. I was pleased also to read about his granddaughter Lisa (Mike's sister), who was in her second year at the University of Arizona studying to be a news photographer.

> As we watch our other ten grandchildren from a distance, who have now become teenagers, they all seem to be eager students. I pray that God may help them all to keep eternity in their hearts, and to keep their priorities straight in this dangerous world.

He also spoke about a phone call he received from Ruben Juarez, a Mexican medical doctor who wanted to take a group of Christian young people to the rural areas of Mexico to help those in need. Dr. Juarez wanted to know how he could get a quantity of Totonac New Testaments. Herman told him they were all sold out but suggested he contact the Mexican Bible Society.

> This might give them a new excuse for printing more copies of the Coyutla Totonac New Testament. If you ask for 500 copies I'll contact the World Home Bible League who have already printed three editions of the Papantla New Testament to see if they will print another 500.

Herman said that, to hurry the printing along, Dr. Juarez should phone Chester Schemper, the CEO of the World Home Bible League, to do "some friendly personal persuasion." Herman also suggested the group visit the town of Zongozotla where there is the largest Totonac church as well as the Totonac Bible School in La Union.

> Dr. Juarez did the latter and found more areas of need. May God use this youthful enthusiasm he has stirred

up. Let's pray for them. And this points up a real need for the Totonacs and for all language groups in Mexico who now have different parts of the Bible translated in their languages. The logistics of distribution really requires someone in the field personally pushing this. We, as well as some other translators, can no longer be out among the people we once served. Our job is really not finished until the translated and printed Word is actually in the hands and used by the people who need it.

I smiled and said "Amen" when I read this at the conclusion of the first page of Herman's letter. But when I flipped the page, I was greatly startled and saddened at what I read.

*Herman and Bessie Aschmann celebrate
fifty years of marriage.*

18

A New Challenge

In his July 1994 letter to me, Herman wrote with great pride about the academic and spiritual development of his grandchildren. He then wrote about a development of a different kind that was occurring in Bessie and which saddened me.

> Regarding Bessie, it is now best for me to be with her as much as possible. She can't be depended upon to carry out some of the simplest tasks, no matter how often I show her. Yet, this shadow of progressive memory loss that seems to be gradually taking over does not depress us. God has given us the peace we need in facing this new challenge. Otherwise we are in good health. We have concentrated on good nutrition to do its work in keeping us well and we need little medication. As for her memory loss there seems to be nothing more we can do about it.

Herman concluded his letter by saying it was 110 degrees Fahrenheit in the shade. But despite the heat he had his nose to the computer and was enjoying it. Further, he had just completed the concordance-dictionary of all the Totonac words found in the Coyutla New Testament. A year later, in June of 1995, Herman wrote another newsletter that began:

> Alzheimer's is a cruel disease. In a few short years it has taken away the real Bessie we knew so well. Caring for Bessie requires twenty-four-hour attention. I try to keep the doors secured with lock and key

otherwise she will take off and usually get lost. Once in such wanderings she was attacked by some dogs. At the time it was traumatic for her but it was soon forgotten. Inside the house, danger lurks behind each cupboard door. Two weeks ago she took a swig of some potent cleaning solvent and came running to me in pain. The hospital emergency ward solved the problem. The doctor then gave me a tranquilizer to put her to sleep at nights so I can get some sleep. I do thank God for His helpers nearby as well as my daughter Rachel who lives not too far away and who helps share this burden with me.

Besides caring for Bessie, Herman had the added trauma of knowing Rick's wife Heidi Marie was going through deep waters with a cancer that was attacking her spinal vertebra. Unable to get the treatment she needed in Colombia, she had returned to the States for a drastic treatment of chemotherapy. It was during this ordeal, between 1994 and 2000, that God graciously gave Herman a new challenge that mitigated some of his pain. In his memoirs, Herman said it all started somewhere in 1994 when Jim Watters—then director of the Mexico Branch—showed him a letter from Dr. Schmalenbach, a German medical missionary, who had started a clinic in one of the Highland Totonac villages.

One of the Totonac helpers in Dr. Schmalenbach's clinic was Lazaro Ponce from Zongozotla. Lazaro was in his last year of seminary and told Dr. Schmalenbach the Sierra (Highland) Totonac New Testament that was published in 1959 needed to be revised. He wondered if someone in SIL could work with him to do this. Lazaro didn't mention Herman, thinking perhaps he was now too old for the task. When Herman received Dr. Schmalenbach's letter, he wrote him immediately, saying this was something he had wanted to do for many years. Herman said he was delighted that Lazaro Ponce had such a burden for a new revision. However, Herman pointed out there were a few problems with Lazaro's desire to do a revision of the New Testament.

> First and foremost, Lazaro Ponce has no experience with the intricacies and techniques of Bible translation. Further, a cursory edit of the original translation would not do. What is needed is a complete overhaul with better research on the exegesis than Manuel and I had done on the original in the forties and fifties. Since then, there has been a whole new Christian vocabulary that has entered the Totonac lexicon and we have found better ways to communicate the gospel truth to Totonac minds and hearts.

Herman went on to explain that in the intervening years he, with his Totonac co-translators, had also translated and published the Papantla and Coyutla Totonac New Testaments. And since these are related languages, any good solutions they might find in one of them might also lead to better solutions in revising the Highland Totonac.

> What I thought I should do first by myself was to examine, verse by verse, the three different New Testaments as source material and make my own draft of a new and more dynamic version. I would be careful to use only correct Highland Totonac grammar and idiomatic expressions to see what I could come up with. Lazaro could then use my better researched version as a base to edit and improve on.

With those plans in mind, Herman soon had Matthew's gospel revised. He then sent six computer printouts of his revision to Totonac speakers he knew in the towns of Mecatlan and Zongozotla, as well as one to Lazaro via Dr. Schmalenbach. He also sent a copy to Felipe Ramos in Nanacatlan.

I wanted their input to tell me how well I was doing. Then in the midst of this, Dr. Schmalenbach wrote to tell me that Lazaro had graduated from seminary, gotten married and was now the pastor of a church in the city of Puebla. And since he now had other priorities to deal with, he would have no time to revise that New Testament with me.

As sad and disquieting as this news was, Herman was in no way deterred from his desire to revise the Highland New Testament. On the contrary, the events actually activated him to continue the revision with all haste.

I felt God must be in what I had started to do. Therefore, I knew I must keep at it until I had finished revising the whole New Testament with my own tentative version. I just had to believe help would come from some other competent mother-tongue Totonac who spoke Spanish well and who would be willing to read and rework my drafts.

In January 1996 Herman finished his revision of the whole New Testament, but he still hadn't received the feedback he wanted from those to whom he had sent the revised copies of the Gospel of Matthew. Meanwhile, Herman had been keeping Dr. Bob Bascom, with the United Bible Society, aware of his progress. Since the 1959 original translation had been a UBS project, they were willing to take this revision as one of their own projects. At the same time, Herman knew his efforts might be in vain if he couldn't find a competent Totonac co-translator to work with him.

While wondering who might help him, Herman was greatly encouraged to receive a large financial gift designated for his revision project. Then, in January 1996, Ken Bowyer with the Unevangelized Fields Mission (formerly Mexican Indian Mission) phoned to tell him that Antonio Hernandez, a Totonac speaker from Mecatlan who had studied at their Bible school, wanted to come to the States to help him. The day before Antonio was to arrive in Mexico City for the SIL office [49] to help him get his passport and visa, someone phoned the office to say Antonio had gotten sick and could no longer come. But all was not lost. Three days later, longtime friend Dr. Dale Kietzman, director of Latin American Indian Ministries (with offices in Southern California), phoned Herman to ask if he would like Felipe Ramos and his wife Lola to come to Tucson to work over his New Testament drafts. The Latin American Indian Ministries had helped support Manuel Arenas for many years with his Totonac Bible School. Dale Kietzman said he would pay their plane fares.

> My joy knew no bounds as no one could be more able to help me than Felipe Ramos. That is how the Lord worked it out so that on February 15, 1996 there were Felipe and Lola nicely settled in an apartment just a block away from our house.

> I immediately sat him down at my notebook computer and with a few instructions on how to use it, he was busily reading over each word of my version trying to find the weak spots to make the text more grammatically correct and an easier understandable rendering. When Felipe made a change in the text, I asked him to clue me in by adding four periods at that place so that when I reviewed his work on my computer, I could discuss his solutions with him. I told him only he, as an intelligent native speaker, could be the ultimate critic as to wording and intelligibility. At first Felipe

---

49 After the SIL Tlalpan property and office buildings were returned to the Mexican government, the pressure from the press diminished. To accommodate those who had permanent papers and those coming in and out of the country on short-term business, SIL maintained a small office and guest house.

was reluctant to make the needed improvements. But before he was half way through, he had gained confidence in finding better solutions than mine. When he realized that, he told me he wanted to start over again and read it a second time. What he learned on his first reading would now help him do a better job the second time.

Herman said it was when Felipe did his second reading that he really began to shine.

When Felipe finished his second reading, he began reading it through for a third time. However, when he got to John's Gospel, he decided there were no longer enough corrections or improvements he needed to make. Anyway, Lola was getting homesick for her children in Mexico.

Dr. Bob Bascom, who had monitored Herman's progress from the beginning, made one last check and was satisfied the Highland Totonac revision was worthy of publication. But Herman wasn't free of problems. In a May 29, 1997, newsletter, Herman wrote:

The United Bible Society had authorized the Mexican Bible Society to publish the New Testament, which they would have done. However, because of severe financial setbacks they have sent us their release so that others might now be allowed to publish it. I have been told that it will take over thirty thousand dollars to print this revised New Testament. Please pray with us as we humbly ask God to help those involved.

In keeping with his character, Herman had actually begun his May 29 newsletter with a prayer request, not for himself but for his son Rick and his three grandchildren—ages 15, 13, and 11. After five years of constant pain, Rick's wife Heidi Marie had died of bone cancer.

> Just before Heidi Marie died, Rick phoned and asked me to come. It was good I did because a week later, two days before the 27th of April when she died, Rick broke his arm up high enough so that it could not be put in a cast. Rick's arm was held in place by a sling. In spite of her suffering, bedridden Heidi Marie had, before she died, continued to answer letters to sympathizers and to those who had phoned her. This was her opportunity to turn the tables on them and be the comforter instead of the comforted! In spite of now being a single parent, Rick is praying that God will allow him to return to Colombia to continue the translation work among the Yukpa people.

On Saturday evening after the funeral, Herman received yet another distressing phone call. While he was in Rick's apartment with his family that included Rob, Tim, and Dan who had come for the funeral, Herman's daughter Rachel called from Tucson.

> Rachel told me that in the nursing home Bessie had fallen and broken her hip. She would have to be operated on the next morning for a hip replacement and could I come back. Here I was on the horns of a dilemma. How could I leave Rick so soon? I was the only one who could drive a car for them. Rick's daughter had also broken her arm a month before.

In consultation with his sons, they all decided it was best for Herman to go back to Tucson. Before Herman left, Rick spoke to his doctor to ask if he thought he could drive. The doctor said yes but warned him to be aware there was the possibility of accidentally damaging his broken arm. Rick decided to take the risk. From his last phone call to Rick, Herman reported that Rick was doing just fine and that his daughter was well enough to drive.

In the same newsletter that told about Heidi Marie's death, Herman reported on Bessie's condition.

> Bessie looks so very tired and haggard. When I go to see her she can't talk and shows no sign of recognizing who I am. She has to be spoon-fed and insists on walking, but her caregivers fear she will fall again unless someone walks with her.

Herman ended his letter by saying that he now lives alone in his mobile home. And that he keeps working on his computer. Some of his projects included enlarging his Highland Totonac-Spanish dictionary (he had already done one for the Coyutla dialect). And to make sure he had enough work to do, Herman had received a request from Campus Crusade for Christ in Canada to translate a first-draft script into Highland Totonac of the "JESUS" film.

> Campus Crusade Canada has had good results in getting the spoken parts of this English language film lip-synchronized to fit the same message in other languages. This will indeed be a challenge to get the complete message to come out effectively in Totonac. Some of the words are extremely long.

One of Herman's rather tender and charming trademarks was the way he signed his letters. Usually each was different and seemed to be a reaffirmation of his love for people and trust in God's sovereignty, even when life was the bleakest. Some were almost brief benedictions. The following are a few examples: "Thank you, God, and to all as well"; "Wishing God's best for you"; "In our Lord's service"; "From someone who loves you all in the Lord"; "Appreciating more and more God's goodness"; and "Appreciating God's love and yours too." A year later, on May 19, 1998, Herman signed off his newsletter with, "Yours As we Try to be Thankful [anyway]." It turned out that on March 12 of that year, Herman was unwisely standing on top of a rickety folding ladder, and, in his own words:

> I was too absorbed in what I was doing to know better. The next thing I knew the ladder doubled up and I fell crashing to the ground with my full body weight on my right hip. I knew immediately something was wrong. I couldn't move my leg. After much calling, someone heard me and I was whisked off to the hospital. I had broken my hip and needed a replacement. How grateful to have my daughter Rachel visit me that very night just before the operation. After ten days in the hospital and rehab I was walking again with the aid of a walker, and wanting badly to go home.

But the powers that be wouldn't release him until he assured them someone would be there at home to care for him. At that point, Herman's son Dan and his wife Diane, who live in Longmont, Colorado, knew they had to do something. Since Dan couldn't be away from his work, Diane and their youngest son Michael flew to Tucson to be with Herman for a month. Whether it was their cheerful presence, or God working in his body in a special way, or both—Herman didn't know—but two days after they arrived he put away his walker and cane and began walking on his own. In November Herman reported that he went every Friday to see Bessie in the nursing home. But by all accounts it was a fruitless visit.

> She will invariably be sleeping in a wheelchair. It takes some doing to get her eyes open and keep her awake. I like to tell her all that is going on in my life and in the life of our family. I hope and pray her benumbed

mind can process some of what I tell her. She can't talk and her eyes don't focus. I think I may have lost her for good as far as this earthly journey goes. At home I feel lonely without her. At the same time, I am thankful for useful things to do on my computer. On Thanksgiving I'll be having the traditional meal with our daughter Rachel. She lives thirty miles from here and also lives alone. We need each other.

A year later, in July 1999, Herman reported that his hip replacement had left him with only a few minor handicaps. He also said he had a cataract operation on his right eye and was thankful he could see much better.

Old age has its compensations and with God's help, I am determined to take advantage of them all. They are part of my learning process on earth. I want to come out with a passing grade.

Appreciating more and more God's grace,
Herman

The church in Coyutla receives the New Testament for the first time with great praise and thankfulness for God's Word in their own Totonac language.

19

The Best Is Yet to Be

It happened in 2000 on his eighty-sixth birthday. On that day Herman learned the revised Highland New Testament had been printed, and 4,000 copies had arrived in Mexico City. In 1997 when the Mexican Bible Society could not publish the New Testament because of lack of funds, the Bible League was happy to become the publisher. Herman learned that some of Felipe's friends in Mexico took 300 copies out to him in Nanacatlan for a special dedication service. On the day of the dedication, hundreds of Totonac believers came from nearby villages to praise God for the New Testament revision. All 300 copies were sold that day. Since then, the rest have been sold.

Here is something interesting about that revision that points out the subtle differences between languages that even the most careful of foreign investigators might not readily catch unless they are well saturated with the language. When Manuel and I worked on the original translation I soon became aware of the variety of nouns that one can derive from the same verb stem in Totonac. So, of course, I took full advantage of this. Whenever there was a noun to translate, Manuel knew what I wanted and gave me the right noun to go with a given context.

Alas, in concentrating on the nouns, I had taught him incorrectly. What I should have become more aware of was that the Totonac language prefers to use verbs in place of nouns much more than Spanish or English. The reason for this is that in Totonac there is much more information in a given context that can or must be included in the verbs of that context than in English or Spanish. It would be boring to explain the ins and outs of this. What I can simply say is that my habit of translating a noun every time there was one in Spanish made for the construction of awkward or heavy sentences for Totonac. That, of course, made for heavy and laborious reading for a Totonac reader. In the revision, Felipe did not have me looking over his shoulder to lead him astray. He knew what a good Totonac sentence should sound like and that is what he was after. If it meant changing nominal ideas to verbal ones, he had the freedom to do so and change them he did.

For many, the year 2000 was marked with millennial excitement. For Herman it was a year of mixed blessing—joy and sorrow.

There was, of course, the great joy in February of finally seeing the revised Highland New Testament received by the Totonac believers with such enthusiasm. Then came March 15.

> On March 15th our son Rick, whose wife Heidi Marie died of cancer three years ago, was married to Betty Unruh. All of his four siblings were there with me in Kearney, Nebraska to see them become one. They will return to Ecuador where Betty will continue working with HCJB, the short wave radio station with a world-wide outreach.

> And now, news about Bessie. During the past nine years I have gradually seen Bessie's personality disintegrate to where she outwardly seemed like a non-person. When I go to see her each week at the nursing home, she is usually sitting in a wheel-chair with a blank emotionless face staring off into nowhere. She can no longer talk. The real Bessie many of us knew so well is no longer there. Last week she could no longer eat or drink and she had to be put into hospice. All we can do now is to wait for that day when her spirit will be released from her body and the real Bessie will make her presence known again in God's presence.

This happened sooner than Herman expected. At three o'clock the next morning, on March 16, God mercifully took Bessie home to a better place. At her memorial service, Herman reminisced about how he first met Bessie in 1940 in Mexico City.

> I didn't get to know that other wonderful side of Bessie until I heard her sing. She had a clear plaintive tremorless voice that made me want to hear more. She

would sometimes accompany herself with her little autoharp. We were married in 1941, and together, she with her autoharp, and I went to live with the Totonac Indians. And as they say, the rest is history.

In November 2000 Herman wrote another newsletter to tell his friends that, as of September, he had moved from the SIL center in Tucson. He was now living in brand new Wycliffe elder-care apartments in Dallas, Texas, with some forty other retired Wycliffe missionaries.

This is indeed an elegant building nestled away among the trees. The Wycliffe Associates came from far and wide to build this lovely place for us. They saw there were now many of us Wycliffe Bible translators getting old and a bit the worse for wear. We needed a comfortable place, just like this one, in which to retire and where we could live together and be of help to each other. So, for a number of years each winter, those eager builder types have been coming in their motor homes while they work at giving the final finishing touches to our retirement home. We will never be able to adequately thank these unsung heroes for their labor of love on our behalf. They indeed have been endowed with the "gift of helps" written about in the twelfth chapter of 1 Corinthians.

While Herman's letter was upbeat, this move was not a happy one at first. When I asked Herman's son Dan why his father moved from Tucson, he said it was because the people at the Catalina center were too busy and he really wanted to retire where he could have more social interaction. He loved Tucson, but the people there who were "retired" were really not retired and continued to do work at the translation center. He thought the Cowan Apartments would be a more socially friendly place for him.

But when he first moved to Dallas, he was disappointed because he said people tended to "live behind closed doors." As time went on, however, he got to know most of the people there and said he really enjoyed having his morning coffee with his friends. Dan continued by saying that his father was still active, reviewing various new translations such as the Coyutla revision that was printed and dedicated in 2007.

> My father still had his computer and was actively involved in watching the phenomenal explosion of the gospel throughout Totonac country spurred by Felipe's radio program. 900 churches!! Can you imagine?

> However, there were some difficult times at Cowan. Dad has always been an eccentric person and many at the Cowan Apartments looked at him as an oddball. He had his vitamins, which were famous in Wycliffe. He had his special foods, which the other residents thought bizarre. His clothes were probably decades old. While going through his stuff, I found an alligator skin belt circa 1950s! Unfortunately, there were some who complained publicly about his eccentricities. That deeply wounded my father. He was such a kind man and it hurt him that people would dislike him because of his behavior. One incident sent him into a period of anger and depression. Some well-meaning older ladies decided he needed new clothes and went out and bought him some. He told me, "How dare someone buy me new clothes? What I wear is my business."

> However, he was also viewed by the younger members of Wycliffe as somewhat of a legend. I recall going to the cafeteria with him for lunch one day, and a young

couple sat down at the table with us. During the conversation, a man introduced himself to my father. When he discovered he was speaking with Herman Aschmann, he got very excited and yelled at the other SIL students in the cafeteria that here was the famous Herman Aschmann. This adulation happened on several occasions. Somehow Dad's early history of translation had taken on historical proportions among some of the young in SIL. Dad never understood it.

In his memoirs, Herman said that when he moved to the Cowan Apartments he wished that Bessie could be there to enjoy it with him.

There is a lot that goes on at the larger Linguistic Center here that this building is a part of. It's like being thrust into a hive of busy bees. Many of those here are new young Bible translator recruits, getting their linguistic training. Seven months have now gone by since Bessie went to be with Jesus, yet in spite of all the good fellowship around me, I still have my times of loneliness for her. I know what she would tell me if she could. It would be: "Herman, give it all you've got. Live only for Jesus! There is a purpose for you being where you are. Make good use of it." Yes, and that is what I'll try to do. The best is yet to be!

Herman concluded his memoirs by first recapping a basic spiritual discipline and then remembering some key people who had been his mentors and to whom he was indebted.

In one of my general letters, I mentioned trying to get into the habit of setting aside a few minutes a day just to think of things I should be thankful for. I haven't been consistent about it, but resurrecting memories of the forgotten blessings of the past has indeed helped me. Especially the past that has to do with those many wonderful years we lived in Mexico among the Totonacs. Bessie and I owe so much to so many Totonacs for the way they wanted to help us. To mention them all would take hours but I'll try to squeeze some of the highlights into a few sentences.

Let me go back to 1939 to Tetelcingo at Uncle Cam Townsend's house where I met my first Totonac. His name was Vicente Cortes and he was already a true follower of Christ. I owe a lot to him for starting me off on my learning to speak his language. But what I owe most to him was for his invitation to go to his home town of Zapotitlán, to live with his mother and five siblings. I did just that, and the six months I lived in that large one-room house with them was a great learning experience. They gave me their only bed to sleep on while they slept on their mats on the floor.

In 1941 Bessie and I were married and we went out there together. It was then that Manuel Arenas entered our lives, and after he came to know the Lord he gave us twelve years of his life to be at my beck and call as we kept working on the translation of the New Testament into his language. He never would let us pay him a cent for all those hours he spent with us. He said God wouldn't let him.

Next we owe a lot to Florencio Jimenez whom God gave us to help translate the New Testament into his Papantla Totonac Indian language. He committed his life and eternal salvation into Christ's hands in Ixmiquilpan at a native writers' workshop. I presented the challenge to him, and he also committed himself fulltime to produce, by himself, a first draft translation of the New Testament into his mother tongue. He gave us five years of his life and almost succeeded, but when he had finished 1 Peter, he was murdered. His brother Jose insisted on taking his place and he gave us much of two years of his life to finish the last six books.

We owe a lot to Padre Jose Rodriguez who put a table at the door of his Catholic church in Papantla to sell the printed Gospels of Mark. He also passed his enthusiasm to sell them on to the other five priests of that Totonac-speaking area. As we printed the other Gospels, as well as Acts and Romans, it was mostly these priests who sold all 7,000 of those little "Good News" books to the Totonac population they ministered to.

Next we owe so much to Padre Jose de la Luz Silva in the town of Coyutla for insisting that we translate the New Testament into his dialect of Totonac in conjunction with the United Bible Societies. It was then that Agustin Juarez, one of the priest's catechists, came into our lives.

He and his wife Micaela gave six busy years of their lives to produce their draft translation of the New Testament in Coyutla Totonac. Padre Silva donated two hundred dollars of his own money for Agustin's wages until a Bible class in Mexico City volunteered to take that on. Then in 1982, Padre Silva suddenly found himself in jeopardy of losing his job if he continued to cooperate with SIL on our translation project, but he finally took the risk and allowed Agustin and me to finish.

Last of all I owe a great deal to Felipe Ramos for coming to the States to help finish the revision of the Sierra Totonac Testament with me. Like Manuel he wouldn't take a cent from us for all his years of working with me. So you see, I owe so much to so many of God's special children who helped Bessie and me as we lived those many years with the Totonac Indians. As I look back over these years I often have said, never give up. Often God's most special blessings come to us as little surprises. The best is yet to be!

Love ya'all,

Herman

Afterword

By way of one last tribute to Herman Aschmann, I have included five people who knew this humble man of God, and who, in one way or another, were blessed and touched by his person and ministry. The first is Felipe Ramos, the voice of the successful Totonac radio program. Herman called Felipe "a wise level-headed scholar and the one who held Manuel's Bible school together."

The second tribute is from Ruth Bishop, a fellow colleague who was allocated by Herman to her Totonac tribal area. The third is from Herman's son Dan, who expresses his love and admiration for his father in spite of inheriting symptoms of his father's ADHD.

And lastly, Dr. Ben Elson, Herman's former Mexico director, and Dr. Eugene Nida both pay Herman the ultimate compliment as an outstanding linguist and Bible translator extraordinaire.

"A Life of Light to the Totonacs" by Felipe Ramos, Co-translator

I am sorry I cannot be there [at the funeral] in person because of the distance that separates us. Nevertheless, I would like to share some words about Mr. Aschmann. He was a spiritual father to me. From the age of ten he began to speak to me about God. He invited me to sit at his table and share his meals and live with his family. He showed me much love. Through the years he invited me to co-labor with him in the translation of the Totonac New Testament. During this time he would ask me for the meaning of every Totonac word. I just thoroughly enjoyed being at his side.

Whenever we would begin work, he would pray for me that I would accept Christ, even though I didn't understand at the time what he meant by that. We would take portions of the Gospels and translate them. Whenever we would finish a particular passage, he would have me read it back with a loud voice to see if there was anything we needed to correct. By the time I was thirteen I was able to confidently read the scriptures that Mr. Aschmann had translated.

Often he would hold meetings in his house to pray and read the Word of God in Totonac. I remember well when during one of those meetings he asked me to give the talk because I could read Totonac well. And so I obeyed, and talked with such passion that I don't even remember what I talked about. I so appreciate the way in which Mr. Aschmann took on the job of mentoring me.

And so it was that I heard the call of God on my life to go to Bible school and prepare myself for a life of service to my Lord and Savior Jesus Christ. I owe so much to this servant of God that led me in that direction. Years later when I got back from Bible school, the first translation of the Totonac New Testament had been completed with the help of Mr. Manuel Arenas.

In the 1970s, this great work of translation would revolutionize the entire Totonac people and culture through the medium of the Totonac radio program. Through this initial effort, seventy-five Christian congregations were begun in the states of Puebla and Veracruz. These initial congregations have now multiplied to more than a thousand churches among the Totonac people in the area where Mr. Aschmann worked.

In a letter to Dr. Dale Kietzman, Felipe gave the following breakdown of where these congregations were located:

450 churches in the Totonac highlands
250 mission churches in the states of Puebla and Veracruz
200 churches in the Papantla area
150 churches in the Coyutla area
40 churches in Xicotepec
With a total membership of over 8,000 believers

✿

"As I Knew Him" by Ruth Bishop, Friend and Colleague

When I think of Herman, the first word that pops into my head is Totonac. Herman knew the language and loved it. He was always ready to discuss Totonac with anyone who would listen. My colleague Aileen Reid and I first became acquainted with Herman and Bessie Aschmann in 1951 when we were assigned to study the Totonac language. He introduced us to the Totonac culture and language. He was always an invaluable source of information and help. Additionally, he was always easy-going, friendly, and cheerful.

Herman was our allocator, helping us find a friendly village, get a house, and learn a few words. Before he left he built us a worktable with a shelf under it, a bench to sit on, and nailed our packing boxes up as cupboards. We discovered Herman was an early riser. When Aileen and I were only thinking about getting up, we heard Herman's cheerful voice, "Breakfast is ready, girls." What a pleasant surprise for us!

One of my favorite recollections of Herman is his ability to make friends anywhere. While waiting to speak to an official in a village, he would sit on a rock or simply just sit next to a man and begin a conversation. He might ask a leading question and get some valuable information, or he might inquire about the man's family. He had made a friend. We met Manuel Arenas early in our acquaintance with the Aschmanns and were delighted that his Bible school was in the area of our village location. Herman included us on trips to see the property and progress on construction. For several years Herman and Bessie lived at the school. Later they had an apartment in Villa Juarez. We had many visits back and forth. Herman stopped at our place en route to or from Tajin when he was working on the Papantla New Testament. He was always generous and willingly shared whatever bits of new information he had learned.

Herman took us on trips, both business and pleasure, to Tecolutla, Papantla, the ruins at Tajin, or to visit another Totonac village. He seldom failed to ask when arriving at our place, "Is there anything I can fix for you?" We were grateful for his help. I can remember holding my breath, though, as he checked for a leak in our butane gas connection. My recollection is that he used a lighted match! But everything was fine.

One morning when we were in the village there was a knock on our closed door and a man's voice called to us in English. We opened it to find our colleagues Hugh Steven and Dick Blight. We were happy to see them and happily greeted them. But Hugh was subdued and abruptly said he was looking for Herman. Herman had paid us a visit the day before but stayed in the town of La Ceiba, our market town. We knew he and Paul Smith were to leave that morning by trail to visit Totonac villages in the highlands.

Then Hugh told us the sad news he had for Herman. His son Johnny had drowned in the bathtub. A dark shadow engulfed our day as we sent Hugh and Dick away, wondering how, where, and when he would catch up with Herman. I know the Lord helped, though I don't know all the details, and Herman was able to return to the family in Mexico City.

When the dedication for the New Testament took place, Aileen and I wanted to be part of the celebration. As we drove our station wagon along the first lap of the trip, I recall pondering the oneness of believers in Christ. In the car were two Canadians: Howard Klassen representing the Mexico Branch, Aileen Reid, my coworker; two Mexicans: the Bible Society representative and a young fellow from a Bible school; two Americans: Herman and myself.

It was a rugged trip hiking all day, climbing mountains—and learning to hang onto a horse's tail for help. We had a wonderful time, visiting Totonacs, enjoying fellowship, the beautiful dedication

service, and wonderful feast. We watched the women making tortillas in an open area, chatted with folks who could speak Spanish,
and enjoyed the brand new outhouse built for the occasion. We were
sorry on the return trip that the lovely lunch sent along didn't get
taken from the pack animal before sending it back! We finally found
a store open and were able to buy a bit of bread. It must have been
close to 11 p.m. when we arrived home. It had rained on the trail,
so we were damp and cold but warm inside with the memory of
that remarkable service that honored the Lord, Herman and his
co-translator, Manuel Arenas, and others who helped make such a
special day possible.

Dan Aschmann Remembers His Father

The ADHD I inherited from my father always got me into a lot of
trouble. Dad's ADHD is an interesting story in itself. A person with
ADHD has neurological wiring that causes many different types of
dysfunctional behavior. Dad told me a lot about his youth and how
his ADHD formed his temperament and personality for functioning
in adulthood. A person with this makeup can never really be a suave
and debonair person. They are "jerky" in their personality, relation-
ships with people, ability to follow instructions, ability to focus and
sit still (even in adulthood). They are characterized by periods of
extreme frustration due to not understanding how everyone around
them seems to be so stable and smooth and they are constantly zig-
zagging and up and down. A person with ADHD needs a strong cause
to give them direction.

Translation was the thing that probably saved my dad from a life-
time of back-to-back failures in life. Dad once recounted to me how
he "really" got into translation. After being Hubel Lemley's partner
for a year, he returned to Mexico City to figure out what to do next.

He told me that because his outward appearance and behavior was unpredictable and seemingly immature, due to ADHD, most people around him didn't put a lot of weight in his ability to be a real translator, not even Uncle Cam. Then when the family that was working in the Highland dialect of Totonac had to return to the U.S. (Landis and Gerdis Christiansen), Uncle Cam casually suggested that if Dad didn't have anything else to do, maybe he could take a look at the work already done. So, Dad sat down with the material and started to go through it.

Dad says that up until this time he had never been good at anything. He described himself has having a "Charlie Brown" childhood with few successes or accolades. He says he never could do anything right, either socially, academically, or athletically. He had siblings who all were great achievers and very successful in life. He described himself as a mediocre person (he continued to believe this throughout his life). In fact, the very idea that Mom would fall in love with him was in itself a miracle to him. He wasn't worthy.

As he began to work through the Totonac material Christiansen had left something amazing happened. He told me, "I looked this stuff over and slowly began to realize I could do this!" It was a huge discovery. He discovered he had a natural ability to understand and work with unwritten languages. The rest is history. He went on to become one of the great Bible translators of the twentieth century, and that according to some of the greatest linguistic minds of the twentieth century. This difficult childhood and self-deprecating attitude kept Dad from the pitfalls of pride. It never ceased to amaze him that people would praise him for the work he was doing. He never really stopped believing that he was a less than ordinary man. But his discovery of these abilities and his passion for the souls of people drove him incessantly for the rest of his life. He finally laid down the "pen" (computer) when he could no longer see the screen due to macular degeneration. To me this is really the story of Dad. It is the idea that God uses those who are most usable.

Dr. Benjamin Elson, Herman's Director in Mexico

In addition to his amazing accomplishment of producing three Totonac New Testament translations, with the assistance of his co-translators, Herman was a very good linguist. He was very perceptive about the structure of the Totonac language. He published on the phonemic system (1946), categories of smell (1946), affixes and implicit categories (1952), and compound verbs (1953). His dictionaries of Highland Totonac (1956, 1962) and of Papantla Totonac (1973) were well received by the Totonac people and also by the academic world. Appendices to the Highland dictionary describe verb structure, numeral classifiers, body parts, etc.

Interspersed with the Totonac work, Herman served the Group (SIL in Mexico) as Government Man (now Director of Public Relations) and also took teams out to where their assigned language is spoken to introduce them to local authorities and to help them get their supply lines established and get started on learning the language.

Dr. Eugene Nida, Herman's Former Linguistics Teacher [50]

There is a tendency to accept academic training as a criterion of expertness in translating, since people think of translators as language professionals and professionalism is usually judged in terms of years of study. On the other hand, one of the most creative translators I have ever known was Herman Aschmann, a person of limited academic training, but one who became entranced by the cultural

---

50 Dr. Nida was one of the greatest linguistic minds of the twentieth century.

content and literary potential of Totonac, an Indian language of Mexico. Instead of submitting one possible rendering of a biblical expression, he usually had a half dozen different ways of representing the meaning of the Greek text. Not only did he produce an exceptional New Testament in Totonac, but he inspired local people to imitate his skill in discovering more and more meaningful ways of communicating a message into an entirely different language and culture.

Postscript

When I finished writing this book, I received a letter from a longtime friend and colleague, Bob Chaney, who wrote: "Herman would rejoice with us that the Totonac people of Veracruz, Mexico are excited at having the New Testament he translated for them now available on the Internet." I also wrote Herman's son Dan and asked him to fill in some blanks about his father's last days, and this is what he said:

> Around 2001 I realized Dad was soon going to leave us and with him would go a lifetime of amazing and invaluable memories. During the week of September 11, 2001, I visited Dad in Dallas. Our plan was to fly to New York City on the 11th to put Mom's ashes to rest at the Aschmann family site. We were just about to leave the apartment for the airport when we saw horrific pictures of the planes flying into the twin towers.

> Instead of going to New York, I got to spend the week with Dad. During that week I essentially commanded him to stop work on translation and change all his energy to writing his memoirs. He complained that no one would read them. I told him his children would at least have a complete firsthand record of his life. I told him we didn't want him to go out without leaving that remembrance. He agreed. What followed was a huge new infusion of energy and purpose in Dad. He dove into the memoirs with gusto and completed them in about a year.

> Finally he could no longer see well enough to use his computer. Macular degeneration removed his ability to do anything but read large print books. This is how

he spent most of his time. When he could no longer read his emails, even with large print, he began to rapidly decline physically. That was about 2004. He now had a lot of friends around him at Cowan and rebuffed all our efforts (and the efforts of Cowan residents) to get him into an assisted living facility. He insisted he was okay. He said he wanted to die in the Cowan Apartments. However, that decision was taken out of his control. Because of his physical decline, he stopped taking care of himself or walking to the cafeteria to eat. After a week of not eating or drinking much, he fell and broke his hip due to weakness and dehydration. His fall also revealed to us and everyone around him that he was in an intermediate state of dementia. This dementia accelerated with the sedatives used at the hospital and recovery center. Finally we brought him back up to Longmont, Colorado to be in a very nice care facility. He passed away four months later on his birthday, February 18, 2008.

Appendix

Reflections on the Death of a Friend

"Out of this matrix of landlocked culture has come the hybrid, Manuel Arenas, who in his 38 years has become a legend among the Totonacs and in more than 25 countries of the world. He is a man I am proud to call a personal friend."

I wrote that in the introduction of my first book, *Manuel,* published in 1970. On May 27, 1992, at 1:30 p.m. my friend died. He was, I think, 60 or 61. No one really knows how old he was. Manuel was born in an obscure mountain village in the highlands of the state of Puebla in southeastern Mexico. In those days, and in such places, few Totonacs recorded the birth of their children. Almost no one could read or write Spanish, and of course no one could read or write Totonac. In 1932 Totonac was one of over 200 languages in Mexico not yet written.

The task of reducing the complex, long-worded Totonac language to writing would be the privilege of Wycliffe's Herman and Bessie Aschmann. Later, Herman with Manuel as his co-translator would translate the New Testament into Highland Totonac and be a major link in introducing Manuel to the Lord.

Within two weeks after Manuel was admitted to a Mexican hospital for an operation to alleviate what had become chronic back pain, the doctors discovered many cancerous tumors throughout his body. The end of his earthly life came within days afterward. When I was told of Manuel's death, the memories immediately came flooding back to me. My most recent memory was of him marching behind fourteen Totonac and other ethnic students who were celebrating their graduation from the Totonac Bible School and Cultural Center he had founded.

The night was hot, the small church packed, and a fierce tropical thunderstorm, with rain that sounded like buckshot on the tin roof, knocked out the fragile electric generator. By candlelight, with his bronze face glistening with perspiration, Manuel read the names of the students and presented their diplomas. Earlier that day at a special luncheon, Manuel had challenged the students to use the training they had received to help others, to maintain a growing relationship with the Lord, and to be faithful in scripture reading and prayer.

The school with its accompanying ministries was the fulfillment of Manuel's lifelong dream. It was a dream that began as a longing for knowledge about the outside world as he worked barefoot in his father's cornfield on the outskirts of his mountain village of Zapotitlan. Within twenty years after leaving his village, Manuel had earned degrees from several Bible colleges and the University of Chicago, and a master's in education from the University of Erlangen, in what was then West Germany. The latter he did in German, which is one of the five or six languages he spoke.

This quantum leap from a barefoot Indian boy to world citizen is chronicled in two books: *Manuel* and its sequel, *Manuel: The Continuing Story*. In both books I tried to capture the way God led and the way Manuel responded to God's leading. Manuel never considered himself anything more than an "instrument" in God's hands. In every way he was careful to give God the glory, and like his other mentor—Wycliffe's founder, William Cameron Townsend—Manuel avoided all personal boasting.

Manuel loved life and the wonders of God's creation, both to observe and to enjoy. His large flower garden at the Totonac Center reflected that interest. He loved people. He loved to laugh and was always eager to join a group who might invite him for lunch or a late-night snack. Yet always before him was the reality that he was God's servant, and that he had a particular responsibility to exercise his influence for his fellow Totonacs. At the time of his death, he was in the process of persuading bank officials and others, who held notes of indebtedness on behalf of Totonac farmers, not to foreclose. Unusual drought conditions had caused a crop failure, and Manuel was pleading their case for more time.

The memory I cherish most was his eagerness to witness for his Lord. Manuel was a gifted personal evangelist. At the New York World's Fair, where Wycliffe had a pavilion, he was their chief spokesman. Whenever there was a particularly difficult or cynical person to deal with, the attending staff called on Manuel to intervene. His authenticity as a person, the vibrancy of his faith, plus his unusual logic and winsomeness almost always saved the day.

I remember also his courage and absolute dependence on the will of God. On one occasion, when he was unsure of the outcome of a possible back operation, he said, "By faith, I will go to the States and have this operation. But if I should die or become confined to a wheelchair, I will not blame anyone. If this is the way the Lord has chosen to end my life I will accept whatever He wills for me." The operation was successful, and God chose to give Manuel seventeen more years of life in which many of the ministries of the Totonac Bible School and Cultural Center were solidified and expanded.

The end of his life came as a complete surprise to most of us who knew him. But his life lives on. It lives on in the lives of those who have been trained in his Bible school, in the churches he began. It lives and in the villagers who responded to the gospel message in the Totonac radio programs hosted by Felipe Ramos. Because Manuel responded to the good news and became Herman Aschmann's co-translator, the scriptures are available in Totonac. The legacy is that because the Word of God is—by the Holy Spirit—a living, breathing instrument, there is a continuing story that will be told in eternity.

Index

A

aboriginal
  language, 31, 40
  peoples, 40
Acosta, Carlos, 109
addiction, 17, 19, 96
Amazon Indian Mission, 41, 50
American. See United States of
  America.
American Bible Society, 114
Amixtlan, 2, 4
anthropology, 123, 129, 134
  cultural, 40
Apache Indians, 30
Apizaco, 135
Appleboxville, Pennsylvania, 23
Arenas, Manuel, 66–70, 81–83,
  85–86, 88–90, 105, 109–10,
  114–15, 120, 122, 129–31, 134,
  141, 143–44, 148, 167, 175, 178,
  186, 191, 193
Armenian, 24–25
Aschmann, Elizabeth (Bessie), 61–68,
  70–72, 74–75, 78–79, 81, 85–88,
  90, 92–93, 97–104, 106–08, 110,
  114–19, 123–29, 134, 136, 139,
  143–44, 147–48, 151–52, 154–55,
  161, 164, 166–70, 173–75, 180,
  182, 187, 190–91, 193
Aschmann, Elsie, 9, 25
Aschmann, Johnny
  death, 1, 5, 7, 118, 123, 151, 198
Aschmann, Liza, 9–12
Aschmann, Paul, 9
Ashmann, Wilhelm, 9–10, 12
Aschmann, William, 9
Assemblies of God Church, 164
atheist, 65
Attention Deficit Hyperactivity
  Disorder (ADHD), 16, 24, 29
Australia, 88
Aztec, 106
  empire, 51

people, 44
village, 44

B

Bacone College, 90
Baltic Sea, 10
Baptist, 33–34
  church, 22, 135
  hospital, 55
  minister, 10
Barnard, Christian, 133
Bascom, Bob, 157, 177, 179
Bear, Mary, 87
Bear, Phil, 87
Bentley, Bill, 31, 36, 43–44
Berkeley, California, 62
Berlin
  West, 110
Bersin family, 10–11
Bible, 22, 30–31, 35, 40–41, 62, 68,
  70, 80, 117, 130, 134, 139, 142–43,
  147, 158
  Bibleless tribe, 31, 40
  class, 140, 152, 158, 192
  fellowship, 24
  Gospel, 4, 22, 28, 107, 119, 144,
  148, 152, 159, 165, 176, 189, 192
  institute, 37
  school, 24–26, 85, 107–09, 125,
  129, 134, 143–44, 164, 167, 177
  Spanish, 69, 75, 143
  story book, 129, 166
  Study, 24
  teacher, 23
  translation ministry, 32
  translator, 1, 30–32, 36, 43,
  47–48, 50, 110, 124, 131, 140, 143,
  145, 147, 152, 171, 175, 190
  Word of God, 80, 117, 196
Bienvenido, 5
Bishop, Ruth, 2
Blast, George, 32
Blight, Dick, 2–6, 37, 118, 198
Bogotá, 168

book of Acts, 105, 149, 152, 156, 192
born again, 22, 24, 159
Bowyer, Ken, 177
Boy Scout Eagle
    badge, 17
Brazil, 30–31, 40–41, 50
Briercrest Academy, 116
Bruce, Verne, 37, 44–46, 51
Burgess, Paul, 46
Burlington Railroad freight depot, 26

C

Cakchiquel
    people, 31
    language, 31
California, 12, 62, 79, 140
    Southern, 178
Camacho, Manuel Avíla, 77
Camargo, Baez, 140, 152, 158
Camp Wycliffe, 29, 31–34, 36, 39–41,
    47, 49–50, 52, 62, 80
Campus Crusade for Christ, 181
Canada, 116, 181
Cárdenas, Lázaro, 36, 41, 175–76
Caribbean, 78
Carlson, Ellen, 87
Carlson, Paul, 87
Caronport, Saskatchewan, 116
Castaneda, Juan, 118
Catalina, Arizona, 167–69, 188
Cayapo, 30
Central American Seminary, 109
Central State College, 124
Chapueltepec Castle, 42
Chattanooga, 124
Chavante, 30
Chiapas, 44
Chicago, 25–26
Chietla, 45
Christian, 10, 23, 138
    Armenian couple, 24
    businesss men, 44
    congregation, 196
    educator, 140
    faith, 21
    family, 122
    funeral, 66
    principles, 119

servanthood, 6
vocabulary, 175
young people, 24, 170
Christmas, 21
church, 21–22, 37, 54, 66–68, 70, 86,
    106–10, 117, 123, 125, 147, 151,
    163, 176, 185, 196
    home, 62
    rural, 33
City College in New York City, 25
cobbler, 10, 12
college education, 24
Colonia Tlalpan, 124
Columbia, 168, 175, 180
Comanche Indians, 30
Connecticut, 10
Cortés, Hernán, 51, 67
Cortés, Vicente, 49, 55–56, 61–62,
    65–66, 106–08, 191
Cowan, George, 88, 90
Coxquihui, 119–20
Coyutla, 2–6, 124, 157–58, 162–63,
    169, 181, 185, 189, 192, 196
Coyutla Totonac New Testament, 163,
    171, 176
Crawford, Bob, 125
Crawford, Percy, 22, 24
culture, 40, 57, 73, 97, 123, 134, 168,
    196

D

Dale, John, 107–08
Dallas Bible Institute, 82
Dallas, Texas, 188–89
Dawson, Bob, 78
Day of the Dead, 71
de la Luz Silva, Padre Jose, 157, 192
Denver, 169
Díaz, Porfirio, 74
domestic servant, 11
Don Quixote, 37
Duran, Agustin Juarez, 158–59,
    162–63, 192

E

Easter, 21, 54
    Sunday, 54
Ecuador, 187

Edigar, Betty, 108
Elson, Ben, 35, 115–16
Emperor Maximilian, 42
English, 40, 80, 82–83, 88, 130–31, 134, 165, 181, 186, 198
English King James, 130
Epistle to the Romans, 149, 152, 156, 192
Escolin, 126, 128–29
Eucharist, 145–46
European immigration, 10
evangelical
    born again, 159
    circles, 22
    evangelist, 108–09
    evangelistic
        sermon, 90
        trip, 33
    evangelization, 67
    evangelize, 68
    missionaries, 80

F

faith, 6, 21, 23, 27–28, 32, 35, 38, 76, 105, 139, 145, 152, 154
    journey, 23
    leap of faith, 10, 68
Farson, Allen, 114, 116
fellowship, 24, 27, 82, 108, 113–14, 190, 198
forgiveness, 19, 69, 107
Fountain, Tom, 78–79
Frye, Northrop, 39

G

Garcia, Herman, 136
Garcia, Ricardo, 108
Gerdel, Florence, 87
German, 82, 142, 144, 175
    Yiddish, 10
Germany, 78, 82
Glendale, California, 79
God, 4, 10, 13, 15–16, 19, 22–23, 27–30, 32, 35, 37–38, 40–41, 50, 54–55, 58, 65, 68–70, 75–77, 82, 100–04, 106–07, 111, 118, 120–22, 128, 136, 138–39, 144–45, 148–49, 151–52, 154, 156, 161,
163–65, 169–71, 174–75, 177, 179–83, 185, 187, 191, 193
    as heavenly Father, 19
Gonzalez, Padre José, 147, 156
Good Friday, 54
Gospel of Mark, 105, 139, 141–43, 145–48, 156–57, 192
Gospel Recordings, 71, 86, 110
Grange, Red, 88
Gravette, 34
Guatemala, 31, 37
Guerrero, 41, 45, 50
Gulf of Mexico, 63
Gutierrez, Juan, 126, 128, 134, 136

H

Happy Valley Farm, 33
Haywood, Tom, 34
HCJB, 187
Hernandez, Antonio, 177
higher education, 24
Highland Totonacs. See Totonac
Highland Tzeltal people. See Tzeltal.
Holland, 12
Hollenbach, Bruce, 158
Holy Spirit, 22, 27, 125
Hueytlalpan, 74
Huitzilan, 106
Hull, Mrs., 43

I

immigrant flooding, 10
immigration, 36, 114
indentured servant, 11
indigenous
    church, 37
    co-translators, 167
    groups, 67
    language, 50
    man, 46
    people groups, 30, 36
influenza, 18
    pandemic, 1919, 17
Ingram, Mr., 44
Instituto Linguistico de Verano (ILV), 163, 166
International Business School, 82
Ixmiquilpan, 136–39, 191

Ixtaccihuatl, 42
Ixtepec, 74, 120, 122, 127

J

Jackson, Carol, 43
Javier, Don, 76–77
Jesus Christ, 5, 22–24, 28, 31, 54, 65,
    69, 76, 107–08, 119, 121, 138–39,
    144–46, 153–54, 158–59, 164,
    181, 190–91
    as Savior, 65, 138, 144
    death and resurrection, 54
    new life in Christ, 22
    sacrificial love, 65
JESUS film, 181
Jimenez, Jose, 107
Jimenez, Padre Manolo, 145
John, 156, 179
John Brown University, 123
John Calvin Theological Seminary, 83
Jopala, 5
joy, 11–12, 19, 114, 117, 148–49, 151,
    154, 178, 186–87
Juarez, Florencio Jimenez, 131, 136–
    49, 151–58, 165, 191
Juarez, Ruben, 170

K

Kearney, Nebraska, 187
Kietzman, Dale, 177–78, 196
Kimmel, Mildred, 43
King Charles VI, 51
King James Version, 134, 165
Kuntz, Mildred, 43

L

La Ceiba, 2–4, 6–7, 198
    airstrip, 2
La Union de Iglesias, 108–09, 134, 171
Lacandón, 87
Lake Necaxa, 51
language, 30–31, 35, 40, 45–48, 50,
    53, 57, 61–62, 68, 80–81, 90, 98,
    127, 130–31, 139, 141, 149, 157,
    165, 171, 176, 181, 186, 191
    aboriginal, 31, 40
    foreign, 142

indigenous, 50
mentor, 53
study, 62
unwritten, 31, 35, 40
Laredo, Texas, 36, 41, 158
Latin America, 30, 37
Latin American Indian Ministries,
    178
Latvia, 10
Latvian, 10
    Bible, 28
    family, 23
Leal, Mary, 43
Leal, Otis, 43
Legters, Brainerd, 43
Legters, Eva, 43
Legters, Leonard Livingston, 30–32,
    40, 46
Lemley, Hubel (Lem), 39, 41, 44–46,
    49–50
Levy, Paulette, 164
Lewis, Midlred (Millie), 49–50
Linguistic Center, 190
linguistics, 35–36, 39–40, 57, 90,
    101, 125
    boundaries, 45
    courses, 80, 147
    department, 164
    descriptive, 39, 50
    discovery, 48
    process, 50
    projects, 167
    scholars, 32
    school, 33
    studies, 49
    training, 31, 34–35, 62, 81, 190
Longmont, Colorado, 182
Lopez, Maria, 4–5
Los Angeles, 86, 88, 110
    studios, 86
love, 19, 24, 49, 61, 64–65, 99, 107,
    117, 124, 145, 154, 181, 188
Luis, Mario, 108
Luna, Javier, 75
Luna, Mariano, 108–09, 119
Luther, Martin, 142
Lutheran, 145

M

Madison Square Gardens, 89–90
Manhattan
    lower East side, 10
Manzano, Aurora, 64–65
Manzano, Miguel, 63–66, 75
Marroquin, Mr., 43
Massachusetts Institute of
    Technology (MIT), 24
Matamoras, 164
Mato Grosso, 30–31
Matthew, 156, 176–77
Mecatlan, 2, 4–5, 124–25, 176–77
mechanical engineering, 24, 107
Memphis, Tennessee, 49
Mendéz, Martín, 55–56
Methodist
    missionary, 75
boarding school, 75
Mexican Bible Society, 41, 43, 117, 157,
    163–64, 170, 179, 185
Mexican Indian Mission, 78, 107, 177
    Bible school, 107
Mexican Revolution, 64
Mexico, 1, 10, 36, 41–44, 50–51, 57,
    62–63, 67–68, 74–75, 77–78, 80,
    86, 88, 128–29,134–35, 140, 144,
    148, 162–63, 166–68, 171, 179,
    185, 191
    eastern, 50
    rural, 4, 44, 170
    southern, 45–46
    visas, 37
Mexico City, 2, 5, 7, 36–38, 41–44,
    51, 55, 62–63, 79, 81–83, 85–87,
    90–91, 93, 99, 109, 114–16, 118–
    19, 124–25, 128–29, 135–37, 140,
    144, 157, 162, 177, 185, 187, 192
Mexico State Department, 166
Miller, Vera, 43
Miller, Walt, 43
ministry, 102
    parish, 10
    partner, 149, 167
    pastoral pulpit, 29
    translation, 32
miracle, 13, 115, 145
mission, 4, 40

Bible school, 125
missionary, 30, 55, 75, 78, 175
    English, 44
    evangelical, 80
    Scottish, 30
    speaker, 30
Missouri, 124
Monterrey, 42
Montezuma II, 51
Moody Bible Institute, 25
morphology, 40, 50
mule driver, 4–6, 45, 52, 55, 63–65
Muskogee, Oklahoma, 90
Mycobacterium (MAI), 168

N

Nanacatlan, 66, 93–94, 98–100,
    108–10, 117–19, 127, 129, 134, 153,
    176, 185
Native Writer's Workshop, 136, 191
New Jersey, 23–24, 80
New Testament, 31, 41, 45, 50, 54,
    69–70, 73, 82, 105, 110, 114, 120,
    124, 126, 129–30, 136, 138–40,
    145, 147, 149, 151–52, 154–58,
    162–65, 167–68, 175–79, 185,
    191–92
New York, 10–12, 36, 90, 128
New York City, 10, 24–26
New York Latvian Baptist Church, 12
Nida, Eugene, 29, 32, 40, 80
Nikkel, Josephine, 43
Norman, Oklahoma, 80, 110, 124,
    134–35
Nyman, William G., 79–80

O

O'Brien, Danny, 2
Oklahoma, 30, 33, 90, 110, 124, 134
Oklahoma City, 129, 134
Oklahoma University, 80, 129, 134
Old Testament, 129, 166
Osorno, 5
Otomi Indian church, 139
Ozarks, 32

P

Papantla, 57, 78–79, 107, 124–27, 135–36, 140–41, 143–47, 152, 154, 156–58, 164, 167, 176, 192, 196
Papantla City high school, 140
Papantla Totonac, 124, 126–27, 136, 141, 147, 156–57, 164, 191
    dictionary, 134, 136, 143, 164
    Gospel, 148
    New Testament, 107, 164
    translator, 164
Paseo de la Reforma, 42
Patla-Chicontla Totonac people, 2
Pearl Harbor, 77
Pentecostal Bible School, 23
phonemics, 40, 130
phonetics, 40
phonology, 50
Pike, Evelyn (Evie) Griset, 29, 34, 43
Pike, Kenneth L., 32, 80
pilot, 3, 6
    bush, 2–3, 6
Pioneer Mission Agency Inc., 80
Piper Cub airplane, 3, 125
Ponce, Lazaro, 175–76
Popocatepetl, 42
Port Chester, New York, 10, 12, 26, 36, 90
Poza Rica, 2, 79, 125, 135, 148, 164
prayer, 67, 90, 104, 121–22, 152, 154, 166, 179
Presbyterian church, 32, 86
Prohibition, 18
Protestant Church, 138, 145
Proverbs, 166
Psalms, 166
Puckett, Doris, 124
Puckett, Larry, 124–25
Puebla, 55–56, 62–63, 78–79, 109, 176
Putnam City High School, 134

Q

Quetzalcoatl's Palace, 82

R

radio program, 22, 148, 167, 189
    gospel, 28
Ramo, Severo, 108–09
Ramos, Felipe, 66, 72, 105, 108–09, 129, 131, 148–49, 167, 176, 178–79, 185–86, 189, 193
Redding, Mike, 170
Reid, Aileen, 2
Revelation, 155–56
Ridderhof, Joy, 71, 86, 110
Riga, 10–11
Robertson, F. W., 47
Rodriguez, Indalecio, 98–99, 117
Rodriguez, Padre Jose, 192
Roman Catholic Church, 54, 67, 138, 145–47, 158, 163, 192
    beliefs, 138
    doctrine, 145
    literature, 147
    theologians, 145
Russian, 10
    Royal Navy, 10

S

Salvador Presbyterian Church, 86
salvation, 21–22, 69, 77, 107, 120, 152, 159, 191
San Felipe Tecpatlan, 52, 55–56, 58
San Francisco, 12
San Pedro Camocuautla, 120
Santo Domingo, 5
Saskatchewan, 116
Sawyer, Tom, 96
Schemper, Chester, 171
Schmalenbach, Dr., 175–76
Sedat, Bill, 43
Siloam Springs, Arkansas, 32–33, 49, 123
Singer Sewing Machine Company, 44
Slocum, Marianna, 87
Smith, Paul, 1–6, 198
Spain, 51
Spanish, 7, 37, 41, 46, 53–56, 67, 69, 71, 74, 78, 81, 97, 108, 120–21, 126–27, 130–31, 136–39, 143–44, 148–49, 155, 157–59, 163–66,

177, 186
hymns, 70
Spanish Devalera, 130
spiritual experience, 22
Stanford University, 170
Stephens, Lois, 43
Stickney, Elsie, 43
Stickney, Newell, 43
Stony Brook, Long Island, 23
Sulphur Springs, Arkansas, 110–11,
116, 123–24
Summer Institute of Linguistics (SIL),
1–2, 49, 79–80, 90, 109, 124, 128,
134, 136–37, 140, 147, 158, 162–
63, 168, 175, 177, 188, 190, 192
Mexico branch, 1, 37, 79, 113, 115,
166, 175, 198
director, 35, 57, 87, 114
workers, 87
Sunday School, 21
experience, 22
teacher, 14, 22
syntax, 40, 50, 130

T

Tahlequah, Oklahoma, 33
Tamaulipas, 164
Tamazunchale, 42, 107–09
Tarahumaras, 87
Tennessee Temple College, 124
Tetela, 75
Tetelcingo, 44, 49–50, 55, 62, 161, 191
The Aschmann Shoe Company, 12
The New English Bible, 133
The Townsend Group, 44, 79
theologian, 80, 145
Tijuana, 107
Tlacoapa, 41, 45–46, 50
Tlaola, 52
Tlapanec, 41, 44–50
Tlapaneco, 47
orthography, 47
Topazian, Alyce, 24–25
Topazian, Shavarsh, 24–25
Totonac, 3, 6, 51–52, 55–57, 63,
66–76, 78, 83, 86–90, 92, 94–96,
98–108, 110, 116–17, 119, 121,
124–27, 129, 131, 134, 137–39,

143, 145, 148–49, 151, 153,
155–59, 161, 163–65, 168–71, 174,
176–77, 179, 185–87, 189, 191–93
area, 2, 51, 57, 118
dictionary, 53
Highland, 55, 62–63, 107, 114,
126, 136, 148, 154, 158, 167, 175–
76, 181
Highland Totonac-Spanish
dictionary, 181
people, 1
Indians, 50, 62–63, 148, 188, 191
animistic beliefs and practices, 67
language, 47, 52, 55, 57, 66, 68,
73, 97–98, 101, 107, 124, 126, 130,
147, 149, 185–86
Lowland, 125, 152, 155–56
New Testament, 61, 69, 81, 83, 85,
105, 107, 110–11, 113–14, 116–17,
120, 122, 141, 158, 163–64, 167,
170–71, 175
people, 2, 4, 10, 48, 78, 95, 97, 111,
158, 164
village, 4, 51–52, 55–57, 61, 69,
106, 126, 164
Totonac Cultural Center and Bible
School, 85
Totonac Cultural Hour, 105
Totonacapan, 74
Townsend, Elvira, 29, 32, 34, 44, 50
Townsend, William Cameron (Uncle
Cam), 29, 31–32, 34–38, 41,
43–44, 50–51, 55, 80, 114, 191
Trans-Siberian
railroad, 11
Tsikáo, 30
Tucson, 167, 178, 180, 182, 188
Tulancingo, Hidalgo, 51, 135
Tzeltal, 87
people, 44

U

Unevangelized Fields Mission
(Mexican Indian Mission), 177
United Bible Society, 146, 149, 152,
157–58, 162, 177, 179, 192
United States of America, 10

American, 12, 43, 81
  culture, 123
  history, 24
  hospital, 91
  visitors, 74
citizen, 88
University of Arizona, 170
University of Chicago, 82
University of Mexico, 164
University of Nuremberg, 82
University of Oklahoma, 80
Unruh, Betty, 187
unwritten language, 30–31, 35, 40
Uranga, Professor, 44

V

Ventspil, 10–11
Veracruz, 78, 125
Vladivostok, 11

W

Wagner, Glen, 88–89
Watters, Jim, 57, 175
Weathers, Ken, 43
Webb, Mr. (Daddy Webb), 44
Westbrae Bible Church, 62
Wheaton College, 41, 50
Wistrand, Kent, 124–25
Wonderly, William, 146, 152, 157–58
World Home Bible League, 171
World War I, 18
Wycliffe Associates, 188
  of Tucson, 167
Wycliffe Bible Translators, 79–80
  translator, 188
Wycliffe Bible Translators
  International, 88
Wycliffe in the Making, 34
Wycliffe, John, 80
Wyrtzen, Jack, 88–90

X

Xicotepec de Juarez, 2, 144, 152, 196
Xingu National Park, 30

Y

youth evangelist, 22, 88
Yukpa Indians, 168, 180

Z

Zacapoaxtla, 63, 65, 77, 87–88, 92, 94
Zacatlan, 55
Zapotitlán, 56–58, 61–63, 65–67,
  69, 73–75, 78–79, 81–82, 85,
  88, 92–94, 97–99, 101, 106, 108,
  119–20, 123, 126, 191
Zaragoza, 63
Zócalo, 42, 86
Zongozotla, 51, 76, 106, 108, 117, 129,
  136, 171, 175–76

The King's College Library
New York, NY
www.tkc.edu

CPSIA information can be obtained
at www.ICGtesting.com
Printed in the USA
BVHW011634081121
621085BV00016BA/465

9 780878 086191